Table of Contents

Introduction

I have always been attracted to the right thing as far back as I can remember. However, as time goes by and change remains constant sometimes the right thing can become blurred with wrong, and I have been able to identify that it is in these moments of life where you are tested. We all go through battles in life, and this is the story that leads to the most transformative time in mine. My intention for sharing my story is to provide inspiration and hope for others who may be going through the same or similar circumstances. Keep seeking out the right thing, do your work to know your truth, stand in your truth which is who you are, and you will live to see how incredibly powerful and fulfilling that is.

Thank you to all the persons who threw obstacles on my path because you were an important part of my life's journey. Your obstacles helped to develop my character and instead provided steppingstones in my ascension to greatness. Your push sent me into finding myself, my purpose, and in doing so served in providing a tool to serve the masses on their individual life journeys through the creation of this book…….

THANK YOU, Dad, for being a constant in my life and always supporting me!

THANK YOU, Mom, for your words of wisdom!

THANK YOU, Brother, for showing me the importance of being independent!

THANK YOU, Che Che, for your sisterhood & support.

THANK YOU, Daryl, my friend for your encouragement to write!

Chapter 1 – Humble Beginnings

I was born on a tiny island in the Caribbean called St. Thomas. As far back as I can remember my days were filled with sunshine because the island is so close to the equator that the weather is sunny all year round. The smells are too decadent to describe as from early morning the scent of cinnamon in cream of wheat, fried john-y cakes, goat water, or fried plantains would seep out of the neighbor's windows filling the air. My first memories are not just filled with my Mom and Dad but with the three women who were instrumental in showing me the kind of woman I wanted to be, my two Grand Mothers, and my Mother. Most of my time was spent with my Mama (my Mothers Mom) with whom I was so fortunate of having the honor and privilege of knowing. Mama was not only one of my guardians but also my friend, confidant, advisor, academic tutor, and biggest supporter. Coming from Spanish and Caribbean roots her home was always a wonderland of orgasmic food prepared with love. As I grew Mama shared with me the basics of cooking, the love of scary movies, the traditions of holidays that bring out the best in us, the beauty in humility, the importance of using your natural gifts to make a difference in not just my own life, the importance of sharing, loving authentically, and above all loving our Creator.

My childhood is filled with memories of Mama taking me to the Spanish Mass at the Cathedral. There, I was exposed not just to religious beliefs but to being part of a community. After every Mass there would be a potluck and everyone would contribute a dish, eat, and socialize with each other. If anyone had problems the congregation would come together and contribute what they could offer weather monetary, knowledge, or spiritual council. The love everyone shared was nothing that I can ever place into words other than to say everyone looked out for one another as a true representation of God's love for us. In this environment I saw how we can all affect each other and took in all the experiences as I grew and started going to Catholic School. Mama made sure that I went to Catholic School and did whatever was in her power to assist.

Catholic School was thirteen years of my life and gave me a glimpse of what to expect as an adult with the politics, agendas, and tricks people can play. I can literally find something I saw or happened to me that can relate to an experience I have gone through as an adult. But I also had my first relationships there and sense of family. To this very day when I see someone from school it is like greeting a family member you have not seen in a long time even the ones you did not get along with. See, the classes were small which allowed for us to have more one-on-one attention with not just each other but with our teachers. Boy did we have some interesting teachers! If you ask anyone that went to Sts. Peter and Paul School there is one name that has a legacy to this very day and that's "Sister Margret". Sister Margret was tough and if you sat in the front of the classroom, you would need a towel to cover your face from the spit bombs that would pummel your glasses and face. A bit up in age Sister Margret commanded the room but also taught us the history of Catholicism, principles of faith, epic stories of the Bible, and the importance of small acts of kindness. When I was in the 3rd grade Sister Margret gave me the opportunity to be pen pals with another little girl in another part of the world. I even got a letter filled with cookies one time from my pen pal and we shared several letters about our lives. Sister Margret always found ways for us to collect and send funding to St. Jude's Hospital and for years spear headed the after-school program where I would get help with my homework and even be able to create different masterpieces through little arts and crafts. Although her reputation preceded her you could get glimpses of the person behind the hard exterior who was kind and wanted to share her knowledge with us.

It is funny when I was in school, I would sit in class and stare at the clock wishing the bell would ring so I could go home, and it always seemed like time stood still. Fast forward to today as I blink it is the next day and I wish that time could stand still again. Looking back while living in that time I wished to be old enough to be out of school and now that I have been out for so long realize those years were some of the best times of my life filled with field trips, recess, fun, and learning in all areas of life not just academics. I was truly prepared with the time I spent there and learned the importance of perseverance in the face of adversity, being respectful to everyone not just my elders, and teamwork. I remember we were taught that if an adult came into the classroom our teacher would announce the sir name of the person and we had to all stand out our seats in respect greeting the person saying, "Good Morning Mr./Mrs. Name & God Loves You" and now if I refer to some people as Mr. or Mrs. they are offended. But that is a testament to how time constantly changes.

Every month or so the entire school would attend Mass, and the Priest or Deacon would deliver a Sermon that usually corresponded with the message delivered in the Gospel reading prior to and I listened to everyone not knowing how much those messages would truly stay with me. As a young person I would have religion classes as a part of the curriculum and would be exposed to the many teachings of the Bible which would be almost like reading a fairy tale because some of us do not get the most impactful experiences in life until much later and little would I know how much they would be a source of strength for me. There would also be designated times for us to attend confession which is a private session with the Priest where you would confess your sins or wrong doings, ask for forgiveness, receive absolution, and penance which would usually be assigned prayers from the priest to complete privately outside the confession chambers in church. I guess there was something in me that captured the interest of one of my teachers because around the 6th grade I was offered the opportunity to serve as what is known as an alter girl in church. This meant I was selected to train as a helper on the alter during Mass assisting the Priest, Deacon, Bishop, Monsignor, or any other member of the Clergy in attendance. I learned well and for the next 5 years I would serve as a alter girl for Sunday Mass and all School Masses up until I was confirmed which is basically the Church acknowledging your becoming a young adult within the Church, and finally becoming a lay person which is when you are ordained by the church to assist the Clergy members in distributing communion. This was an honor and I served with pride because being involved made me feel a part of something greater than just myself.

Most of my friends growing up were boys and for some time I was a bit of a tom boy preferring to be one of the guys even though I wore a uniform with a skirt and looked like a cute little girl with a ponytail. At heart, I was most comfortable around the guys and to this day that is where I feel the most comfortable. Relationships with girls came around middle school and so came the lessons. Girls would befriend me just to get close to one of the guys I was cool with. And the one guy I crushed on made me deathly afraid of letting him know. So, I made an alliance with one of the girls in my class who agreed to help me because I was close to and could talk with the guy of her interest. My guy just so happened to be one of the most popular in our class and his best friend was the guy of her interest. This plan we came up with apparently worked because eventually my guy mustered up the boldness to come to me and ask to go steady which felt like an out of body experience. The day it all went down we were in line waiting to go into science class and he was next to me, started a conversation, and just dropped the question. It felt like Hiroshima and on the inside, I drew a blank but somehow outside I kept it together and told him yes. Now, what I saw between my Grandparents and Parents Marriages really came into play here because it affected how I acted in that relationship. I would let him come to me and would rarely show affection even though inside all I wanted to do was shower him with it. He brought out my first experience with vulnerability which scared me to the point of no words, and I could never go to my parents or grandparents to talk about it because I was given the impression that I would die if the talk of boys ever came up. So, I was in this alone and while the vulnerability of the relationship was like facing the headless horseman, the more I was around him became addicted to all the affection he gave which would become one of my weaknesses later. Being with him would also make me a target. There was a girl in our class who flat out kissed him in front of me and I just looked and walked away. Understanding why that happened did something to me that was like a shot to my head. Someone could replace me easily, and I had no tangible concept of my true worth as a woman. The relationship did not last long after that, but we still have a rapport with each other to this day. That one relationship set the stage for many after it that would eventually strip me down to the most vulnerable moment of my life. So, after an awfully long time of grieving I finally got back to my old self and started to explore. I took up reading old classics like Romeo and Juliet, getting lost in music, watching a lot of fantasy movies like "Never Ending Story", and even dabbling in some acting for school plays. Eventually, I found one of my passions which was singing and after that I cantered in Mass, became one of the youngest members of the Senior Choir, and was mentored by one of the most respected singers in my Community "Ms. Fay Moon"(God Bless her now resting in peace).

The next relationship in my life would come as I approached fifteen. I met Mr. Potential though my best friend at the time not knowing how significant he would become. In this relationship I would show my vulnerability, and for the first time stand my ground (a concept that I had no full understanding of). It was the one big teen age romance most of us may go through. He made efforts to see me outside of school, called me on the phone, wrote me the sweetest love letters, and invested a lot of his time into getting to know me. However, because I was so protected as a young lady by my parents, grandparents, and uncles we could not go on any dates or be allowed to be alone in any way. This relationship was a matter of right person but wrong timing. While we both came to love each other very much neither of us lived yet. Still, this lasted about three years as he was two years older than me and graduated high school before me. I wanted the best for him so I would encourage him to look at different colleges or trades to get into after his graduation as I was doing the same in preparation for my graduation. I made sure to attend his events like his boxing matches and try my best to be as present as possible given my limitations. As my sixteen-year-old self I felt he was the one who would prove everyone with the wrong idea of him wrong and be the man to create the life he desired making me a part of it and marrying me one day. In this vulnerable state I gave him my **virtue**. We were for a time happy until I learned that he was not only writing letters to me but also to my best friend as well. Not only were letters going to my best friend, but he also confided in me that he had an off and on relationship with a young lady that was several years older than him. This would be the moment where I stood my ground for the first time in this capacity and demanded that any old relationships he had needed to be closed if I were to continue being in his life and he would have to make me a priority. To the best of my knowledge, he kept his word and released the relationships he had before meeting me. At such a young age I also became aware that this is just what some men do, and it is accepted being with multiple women at a time. This awareness just as with witnessing my first boyfriends kiss with another girl created this horrifically damaging mindset that would later be the cause of going into the same or similar circumstances of relationships for the next seventeen years of my life. I would either connect with emotionally disconnected men and over give of myself to prove my worth or connect with the extreme opposite emotionally overwhelmed men. Mr. Potential did not know himself yet and was doing what most men do in search of themselves. I did not understand this as my nature was believing in chivalry, that a woman held value in their eyes, and that men were just somehow defenders of us, protectors, providers, lovers, and friends not knowing the journey they go through to *maybe* one day becoming those things just as women have their own journeys to becoming strong, nurturing, intelligent, and supportive *partners*. Learning that men are with multiple women at a time and that it is just the natural order of things broke something in me. My dream of being the woman that a man fights for was crushed and suppressed where I only held onto it with a sliver of hope. It was this hope that sent me into repetitive cycle relationships and disappointment after disappointment. Mr. Potential and I parted ways after about a year of his moving to New Jersey and joining job corps to find his way in life. This was after I learned that once again, he was seeing someone there in the job corps which was the last straw for me. We still speak occasionally from time to time. He has even apologized profusely over the years and explained to me where his mind was. Experiences can change us through life. I became damaged, broken, and because of how society is structured chose to continue forming connections in the toxicity of being with men who were openly with other women and hoping for the fruition of my dream. The lies came more frequently as I graduated to men who omitted the fact of them being married or just did not tell me their status until it would just be thrown in my face.

The relationship with my Mother has been and I believe will remain a complicated one. My Mom took more of a stance of certain things are just not done or talked about. As a young girl I remember being much closer to my Mom sneaking into my parents' bed and snuggling up next to her just as I did with my Mama, and wondering what Mommy would be cooking for dinner, or planning for Christmas/ my Birthday/Vacations. My Mom was also instrumental in showing me the basics like how to iron my school cloths, how to cook certain things, how to comb my hair, how to wash cloths, and how to organize myself. However, as I became older who I was growing into was not the little girl that thought like, agreed with, or did everything as my Mom said or dictated. The fact that I would be shut down when trying to communicate by being spoken over or told we are not speaking about whatever I brought up of significance caused more strain on our relationship over the years so much so that it manifested in my going into severely depressed states in my teens and thoughts of suicide which resulted in my Mother sending me to a Guidance Counselor who basically told me I was a normal teenager and when trying to speak with my parents came up against that same issue as I was which resulted in no more sessions after that. It would take a lot of time, disagreements, and periods of separation between my Mother and I before I could come to just accept that the areas where Mother and I were different could not be changed, embrace it, and respectfully agree to disagree moving forward was a major part of my healing process later in life. I think of us as vinegar and oil sometimes they are two liquids that do not mix but when you put them together with some herbs make a bomb salad dressing. Despite the differences in character between my Mom & Myself I know that the way I was brought up was out of love and protection especially being my Moms only child and a girl. My Mom is a special person, who brings life to a party, joy with her smile, and ignites deep thought with her words of wisdom. All the best qualities I am glad to admit taking from her in addition to the life lessons I saw her go through and overcome. It would also take years for me to recognize, recover, and heal from the communication issues that manifested as a result when dealing with dictatorial confrontation throughout my life. This would later be one of the biggest lessons of my life with respect to learning how to deal with opposing forces imposing their will on me, gaining confidence, finding my voice, and enforcing necessary respect and or boundaries for myself in all situations.

When I got to 11th grade, I auditioned for one of the biggest shows on the island and was selected to be a part of the show. This was my first experience being around people who shared the same passion as I did. We practiced for months a few days during the week, and every weekend until I became sick. I lost my voice just before opening night. But, I fought, and my parents supported me by giving me bush baths and home remedies to get me back on my feet. Opening night, I slayed my performance, and all other performances for the duration of the show. I loved the experience so much and went back the next year to do it all over again. The exposure to this kind of environment was a huge learning experience. There were dancers, singers, and rappers comprised of kids around my age and adults all with individual performance pieces as well as group performances. I met another crush who I thought was so sweet. This one was the boy next door type who came from a well-respected family in the community and was what every Mom would look forward to meeting. I will refer to him as my "Gentleman" because he exuded all those qualities. Now, it is at that point I noticed starting a pattern. I would mostly sit by him, be the initiator and call him, and even try to go to places or events I knew he would be at. But even though I started liking him in the sense of forming a relationship, he did not but would-be exceedingly kind and sweet about it. Over the years we connected every now and again, but it became crystal clear that we both wanted different things in life. He wanted to pursue a career in the entertainment industry, and I also wanted that, but the deal breaker was that I wanted a family, and it did not appear that kids were in the plan for him. So, after our first and last date a few years later we parted as friends. The next year I auditioned and got in again there was a new group of cast members and I got my first look into the male / female dance that happens. With two groups of dancers, boys, and girls all around my age I saw relationships form and fizzle out, female competition, teen age hormones, and even haters spreading gossip. Yep, that is basically the setting for most places where people on the island meet, work, or go to school, and yes even in church. I also had a crush. And, once again I did the chasing, more aggressively this time. I would give him compliments, watch him, try to make up reasons to be near him at rehearsals, but this one did not like me that way either because his eyes were set on another girl. So, this time around I did not really feel as good as the first time I went into the show, at times I felt like I did not fit in, and I missed my "Gentleman" which was the second pattern I noticed forming around that time. I equated not having a boyfriend or being able to snag one as not being good enough. Going through an experience like being in a show is terrifying especially if it is your first time and my "Gentleman" was like my knight in shining armor, he made the first experience so empowering just being in his presence and having a friend looking out for me. So, from that I gathered that I was not good enough in my own skin being surrounded by fit, talented, young women who were secure in their skin, and me being full figured not as secure in mine. This mind set only got worse and became part of the foundation that created more deteriorating mind sets.

Senior year was a blur! Apparently, I had more than enough credits to graduate which gave me the option to take additional classes or take a few select courses until twelve pm and go on to a school to work program. I opted for the school to work program, worked from 1 – 6 pm during the week and full time on Saturdays. At eighteen I was making what some adults were making every two weeks, I gained my first experience with managing my own money and started my own self-care treatment routine. When graduation came, we all parted ways, some going to the United States to attend different Universities, and others like myself stayed home, took a break from school, went in the work force, or attended the University of the Virgin Islands (UVI), home of the Buccaneers. Most of the more mature influencers of excellence in my life such as close friends of the family encouraged me to continue my education by committing to a program in college. One of the most important influences was my Aunt, Dr. Marilyn F. Krigger Professor Emeritus at UVI (retired), whom is a distinguished Author of literary work on the history of Race Relations in the US Virgin Islands, and a Historian amongst many other accomplishments. Aunty Marilyn ensured to share with me the importance of continuing my education, showed her support in being present at my graduation and many other milestones in my life in addition to gifting me with her support as well. My decision was to continue working and to attend UVI full time. Life changed from living with my parents to living in my own dorm room and making my own decisions. It was this time of my life that I really connected with other young women making several friends. The relationships made were unforgettable even the bad ones. One day I was with a friend at the Ladies singles dorms and was introduced to a young man who looked like one of my favorite singers. There was just something about him that was so familiar, and I liked him instantly. I even remember telling him that he looked just like the artist "Pharell" which would annoy him because I was not the first person to point this out. After this first meeting time went by and soon it was time to re-register for spring semester. While on my rounds of tasks to complete I went to the registrar's office to apply for spring semester and to my surprise I bumped into "Mr. Mystery" again. Since we had already been introduced, we quickly took to each other, started a conversation, and so one of the most important relationships of my life started. Now for privacy purposes I will only refer to him as Mr. Mystery, but he knows who he is. Mr. Mystery became the best friend who never knew how much he held my heart in his hands. Being around him felt safe like coming home for Christmas. That big word "Vulnerability" had found its way to me again and instead of being courageous enough to tell him the extent of my feelings I choose to hide them away and keep things friend zoned, terrified of losing him. Because of this I was there through just about everything, every girlfriend, event, and party. I supported his passions, was his confidant, and he was mine. Mr. Mystery was a man of many talents one of which was the use of his hands. He was the first Artist I had met in person who painted and drew from such dark places. One of his sketches is still etched in my mind, the image of a man both arms bound in chains coming out of the ground while he is trying to free himself.

Now, while I spent most of my free time with Mr. Mystery, I still managed to keep a balanced life going to work, attending classes, socializing, and venturing into travel adventures. When I met Mr. Mystery, he did have a girlfriend and introduced me. The three of us became awfully close, and while we were friends, I could not help but wonder why his girlfriend would be so ok with us being so close and spending so much time with each other. Then the day came that his brother came to visit who let us just say brought up some very naughty thoughts at first glance. We will call him "Stick Man". When Mystery and I became close friends, we realized that we all went to the same school as children. Stick Man and I were both in Kindergarten together and it was interesting to see how he had grown from that shy little boy who would pull my ponytail into this very strapping young man. I guess you could say he was my first man crush, and I was not shy to let him know that he was, within a pg-13 rating though. I loved this time of my life.

Then my world was shaken as my Mama fell ill and my Mom and I would take turns going to care for her until the day I got the call in the middle of the night that she passed onto Grace. There are no words to describe the pain that shot through my body. All I could manage to do was call Mystery screaming and he ran to my rescue consoling me as I cried. Then I managed to pull myself together and go to the Hospital to meet the rest of my family. Everything went downhill from there! I started to drink heavily while Mystery stayed close watching over me and making sure I was safe. He came to the Funeral and stayed with me after. When I would get drunk beyond recognition, he would always make sure to be with me and get me back to my dorm safely or let me crash by him. I could not focus on school, ended up seeing the school counselor and leaving school not too long after that. As I slowly came to terms with her being gone Mystery filled part of that void. We had so many adventures and made so many memories that I put that chapter of my life behind me and looked for the good in my future. I decided to go into hospitality with the intentions of saving some money and going back to school. But that plan did not end up falling through so I dedicated myself to my career and advancement. Technology had drastically advanced and social media was slowly being introduced with websites like my space and hi 5 around that time. So, I created my account and started connecting with people, making friends, and one day came across a very handsome picture. I was bold, reached out, and sent him a message never expecting a response. However, he responded to me. We will call him S. Now, S was so sweet, and I remember the first time we spoke over the phone he played the song "I wanna be your Man" to me. S came from a very prominent Family on the island as well but lived in the United States. Our relationship revolved around phone calls and text messages and when I was making enough money, I would visit him from time to time or he would visit me. Things were not all perfect as no one ever is. S had a lot of emotional issues because of his past and as we spent more time together it became apparent to make the hard decision of moving on. But, through the experience I met my "Bff" who stands by me to this very day. The fabulous one and only "Ms. Che Che".

After S I once again focused on my career which ended up leading me to working for the most prestigious resort on the island in entry level management. I loved my job, was exposed to many of the luxuries of life, and had the opportunity to meet so many different people. My career allowed me to be a part of making memories that last lifetimes and I took it very seriously. However, good things can come along with bad, and I really had my first experience with the tests and trials that come along with working alongside others, how your race plays a role for how certain people advance in careers, and how easily people you work with and think you can count on will easily throw you to the sharks for breakfast to save their own ass. There, I learned the importance of documenting everything to a t after going through unfavorable events with management and even co-workers. During my time there I was charged with operating the resorts lounge at the Airport. There, I met the next Man that would catch my eye. The caramel skin, physique, and authority with which he carried himself won me over in a heartbeat. We shall call him "Mr. Temptation" as this is what he was every time I laid my eyes on him. Every day I would go to work and would have to snap myself out of doting until eventually I maneuvered my way to speaking with him using the avenue of asking questions to know for my job occasionally to strike up a conversation and be noticed. What I did not know was that his eye had been on me as well which was a shock. I grew up hearing my family say that I was beautiful and would even hear it from other people as well but never really thought that way of myself and the fact that I was also full figured for most of my life I looked at myself as there is always someone more beautiful because I was not the perfect weight. Looking back, I did not understand where any of my appeal came from. Because I thought of myself as ordinary, I would attract certain types of men which resulted in relationships with similar patterns. Every time I would go into a relationship, I would allow my mind to be flooded with doubts like I am too fat, this will not last, and he is too good looking so he must have other women. This would be the third most important relationship to shape me while breaking me down at the same time. When I loved I would put the person before me and eventually would do anything I could think of to please. But in the beginning, it was almost perfect. He would also find little opportunities to speak with me, eventually asked for my number, and then came the first date. I was so nervous because this was the first time I was ever asked out and he was older than me by some years while I was still in my early twenties. We met at night on the beach right next to the airport and sat on a bench by the sea. I started talking to open communication and though he listened at first just a few minutes into the conversation I was met with a kiss. Everything was a blur after that and though the night remained innocent that kiss did something to me. I liked him before we started talking but after the kiss, I felt closer. My secret doubts went into overdrive and I made sure I did things to play the part thinking that doing for him would keep him. Being with him opened me up to physical and emotional parts of relationship and I would go to be with him as much as he would allow, offer to bring lunch every day, and yes even offering physical pleasure. This is what I came to think was what kept a man with you and when he started to pull away all my doubts started to manifest. He did have other women, they were skinnier and prettier than I was, and I degraded myself by staying in that. I would offer myself to him, take him to work, do odd jobs, and even resorted to giving him money. He would never take me out in public on a date, and our meetings would always be at night, by his apartment, in my car to take him somewhere, somewhere out of sight, and I stayed in that for about a year until one day after finding out he would be leaving the island for training he asked me to meet him at his apartment. After leaving my night job I drove to his apartment to spend some time with him and give him some money as a gift. When I came into the apartment it was early and the sun was just coming out, he opened the door, led me to his bedroom and as I entered met me with such a deep passionate hug. This hug embraced me and as he quietly held me, I started to get concerned, asked if everything was ok, and I do not think he heard me because he held onto me as if he never wanted to let me go. Then, when I started to break the embrace, he responded everything was ok and asked me to stay. I responded saying I could not stay long because I had to prepare for work soon. So, I stayed for a little while and could tell that for a moment I was wanted. I did not know how to react to that especially after being with him and told not to go falling in love, through the women, the co-workers in my ear about his reputation, and still not being in an exclusive relationship.

I left his place that day not knowing what was to come and just two days later while driving home from work in the early morning my jeeps breaks failed as I turned a sharp corner and plummeted about 40 ft off a cliff. When I came too, I was looking out the window hanging upside down still listening to "Love in this Club" that was playing until the driver of the vehicle I apparently hit came to my aid and made sure I made it back up to the road safely. Still being in a daze I did not realize the severity of the accident until when I looked down at where my car fell then I burst into tears and balled up into a fetal position on the ground. My parents got there quick and stayed with me at the Hospital when I finally calmed down and started to relax. Temptation made it to the hospital just after I was rolled into the emergency room, came to make sure I was ok, stayed for a moment and left. Looking back on that time I remember being in the mind frame of this was just one of those s*** happens in life moments and went into a reactive mode. Once I was out of the hospital, I went through the checks of dealing with the bank, insurance, medical documents for time off with both jobs, and then making the devastating decision of having to let go one of my jobs while taking on recovery. After, I recovered and started working again something in me changed and I was drawn to the idea of moving to the States which I made a reality. Of course, though the move did not happen according to plan I did manage to secure a job as an overnight front desk supervisor and started working just four short days after I transitioned to Fort. Lauderdale.

Chapter 2 – Repetitive Cycles

      Living in Fort. Lauderdale was just the change I needed. The plan was to acquire another job, save for my own place & car, and then go back to school specifically for business management. I had my Duncan Donut & Starbuck mornings, little weekend adventures like learning the public transportation system, driving on the other side of the road, learning how to use the hi way, and even driving up to Orlando one time to visit a friend on my own. However, the job that I was so proud of myself for pulling soon came with conflict. People were secretly putting ideas in Mgmts. ear. I would notice how other employees would "suck up" as a tactic to secure their position after I got invited once to go out for drinks with the team. My candidness and understanding for other employees made me a threat. Once again, I saw the faces that people put on in your face and the knives placed in my back when I would receive my performance evaluation. I stayed in this environment for a little over a year until I took a short trip home to recoup which ended up being extended due to my flight being cancelled, and when I called to give notice, everyone wanted to play the evading game. Eventually, I received contact with the director of the department who basically advised me of my termination. Since it was unfair, I contacted the GM who was willing to work with me to return to work, however I would be placed right back in the same environment, so I thanked him for trying and decided to cut my loses, stay home, and move my things later.

      My living situation also became very toxic which made the decision even easier for me, and it took me a few months, but I was able to secure another Supervisor position in another one of the largest Resorts on the island. Now, by this time I felt a shift in what I wanted to do because even though I was grateful for the opportunity once again I noticed the environment became toxic. I saw how Mgmt. took advantage of me paying me much less than what I was worth, while holding me back from promotion, and delegating more responsibilities on me while covering missing shifts as well. That lasted about a year before I transitioned to another Supervisor/Management position at another hotel where once again the cycle would repeat. This got me to a point of being so tired of the same situation in different locations. And as I look back, I could not see what the actual problem was going through all that transition. While my skills spoke for themselves, and I more than did what was required of me I lacked in emotional knowledge to understand how to interact and move past such conflicted environments. Because I was so focused on proving myself and meeting my personal goals, I suppressed a lot of deep seeded anger, resentment, pain, and feelings of unworthiness due to the trauma of the toxic cycles I kept going into which made me easy prey to be taken advantage of in working environments and relationships. I did not understand how to stand up for myself, stand my ground, or establish boundaries in both the professional and personal part of my life. Nor did I understand what I needed to due to address this repeating cycle. Repetitive cycles also continued in my love life as well. I would constantly meet the same character in different men with only slight differences. If they were not emotionally disconnected, I would be used, or they were too soft and unable to stand ground for themselves much less for me.

While working at the last property I met a certain co-worker whom I came to work very closely with. This man at the time was handsome, but because of where I was in my life, I did not even think of anything occurring between us. Little did I know how deep that tie went. This one went out of his way to bait me offering me transportation home from work, walks to talk, or just hovering around me at work. This would become the second most destructive relationship I would ever be in. I was lied to about him being married and found out once it was too late having already fallen for him. My faults in the relationship would be what I came to see later as me seeking validation by showing what I could do as a significant other through cooking, giving money, doing favors, sex, and doing all the things I thought I was supposed to do to please and keep him. In the years I subjected myself to literal hell in the name of what I thought was love I lost a child while this man had two more children with his wife that he lied about having.

As difficult as it was, I just could not take the abuse anymore and I left that job changing my career completely going into the field of communications. Eventually, I made enough money to pay off my vehicle fly back to the states to settle my affairs, ship my vehicle home, and settle well into another career that I was passionate about. I always had a love for technology and the position I took was a mixture of being an associate / manager on another island. This did not stop the person from finding his way back into my life and he would keep playing mind games making empty promises and harassing me to do favors with nothing in return. Eventually, I made a good enough impression that I got the opportunity to move to customer service with this new company I worked for. I met and was surrounded by some of the most phenomenal women who taught me so much with their professionalism, poise, and empathy which I took and used to grow in this new department. After about six months I was given the opportunity to transfer to a more technical department where I would remain for the most of my time spent in this new company. This finally got me completely away from the last destructive relationship as I was able to cut all communication and ties with him from the move to a new job location.

Now, I did learn from all the backstabbing experiences I had in the past and before I moved down to this new department, I did a really good job at not having friends or getting too close to anyone in the workplace until this move. This new department and the time I spent there would accelerate new toxic cycles in my life that I would later almost die from. However, I will start from the time I entered. I came in bright eyed and eager to learn everything I could again trying to prove myself. There was a lot of strife between co-workers in the department when I arrived. However, I managed to stay focused on getting the technical training I needed to perform and stay out of petty quarrels until the day I was thrown into one. Understand, when you are in a toxic place it does not matter how much you keep yourself separate from others, try to only keep things on a professional level, and see injustices but stay quiet and neutral it will only be a matter of time before people will try you. See, as much as I was looking out for myself by not getting involved, not forming close friendships, and choosing to just be about work the more I would be looked at as a question mark. When your seen as a question mark because you choose to keep to yourself and not disclose much of whom you are personally eventually someone will try you to get a peek behind your vail. The question becomes are you a pushover that anything can be done too or are you a threat? In my case I was a wild card because for the most part I did see a lot of things in that working environment that was certainly not right. I witnessed co-workers being harassed by other co-workers either in office situations of accusations or taking their petty drama and making complaints to the supervisor in back-and-forth arguments of who felt they were right and wrong. The Supervisor at the time I got there was a much older Lady near to retirement with years of experience and did the best in addressing these situations as they occurred until retiring about a year after I came. For about the first two years I was there things seemed to look up for me and I had a sense of financial security managing my own affairs, started planning for my future, and saving enough to move out from my parents' home to a quiet little cottage on the north side of the island. I was independent and loving my newfound freedom at the age of twenty-eight. During that time, I also rekindled a friendship that went sour some years before and we would hang out like old times. Unfortunately, I came to find out who that person really was, and we parted ways again permanently. The lesson I took from that was not every or anyone is a real friend and not everyone will take friendship as I will so this made me close my friendship circle to about a party of four. Just before I let go of that friendship, I received the news that Mystery the man I left my heart with so many years ago was getting married. I was at a loss for words, but I kept it together and congratulated him. However, I was not invited to the wedding, nor would I be included in any part of his life moving forward. This was one of hardest pills I swallowed and before communication stopped prior to the marriage I did manage as best as I could to let him know my real feelings which did not matter and that was made clear to me. What seemed like a lifetime of friendship, memories, love, and mutual respect was just thrown away. The way I delt with that was to isolate myself and my circle went down to a party of three which I would rarely communicate with. People grow, get married, start families, and sometimes move to another country. So, for the first time since I was back in elementary school, I was an introvert again just working, planning to go back to school, and taking care of myself and my family.

Now, after all these major changes occurred at work new challenges came. The state of the department was chaotic under the new supervisor. This is where I started to try and reach out communicating the break downs I was seeing. At first my efforts seemed to be appreciated that is until I witnessed one of my co-workers being harassed / targeted by the supervisor so much that my co-worker got so upset on the job one day and resigned. This allowed for an opening in the department and conveniently the person who would fill it would be a friend of the supervisor transferring in. As this new person spent more time in the department many of the issues being brought to the supervisor would involve this person. And it did not matter what you did or said that person was there to stay, have privilege without having to complete work, come in late, and in some cases do whatever they liked. As time progressed, I would see a lot more issues of concern which mainly led to seeing that this person was also a point man put in the department as a look out for the supervisor and they would regularly stay in communication to keep the supervisor informed on anything that happened while the supervisor disappeared for hours every day. Imagine being in this type of environment for years each year progressively getting worse. Eventually, the two eldest persons in the office retired and this allowed for two new people to transfer in from other departments. Which was a good change, but then in my observations this only made the inner circle apply pressure to weed out who would convert to their side and who would oppose the crap being enforced. The tactics included nepotism, benefits, intimidation through disciplinary action whether trumped up or through micromanagement and overworking those not in the inner circle. I faced a lot of phycological warfare to get me to transition into a work bot while others would have life on easy street and at first, I would bring up the issues I saw only to be met with the attitude that it was not my job to monitor people. There would be little to no change and if there was it would only be circumvented later because the change was just a show to pacify something was done to address the issues I presented.

In between all this going on in my career I met whom I shall refer to as "The Great Pretender". This one was a double lifer, meaning a man living double lives and looking back I was told this but was not really reading into what I was being told. This one spotted me in a plaza as I was driving to the laundry. He made sure to grab my attention by motioning to me to pull over which I did. In speaking with him I was under the impression that he wanted my contact information for "Business" purposes. It would not even be 24 hours before I started getting the text messages and calls almost every day and night. I recognized it as a red flag and I even questioned him later, but my biggest issue was being trusting with everyone. Instead of making him prove himself to me that he was trustworthy. Even though I was acquainted with him for a few years through the careers I held in Hospitality it was only just that a professional acquaintance. So, I trusted in that knowledge of him which was not much to go on. I learned you can be acquainted with a person for years and never know their true nature. Putting on masks and using manipulation is mastered by some people especially looking for their come up! So, the communication quickly turned into us spending time with each other about two weeks later. And this one did not know anything from me other than my number, but he searched me out and tracked down one of my co-workers which is how he was able to start the wooing process by using this co-worker at the time to ask me what I would like for lunch and things of that nature. Now, again looking back on this I saw how I got baited easily. I was not dating anyone at the time because I came out of a horrific relationship and was single for a while, but I did not really start dealing with myself and healing from all I went through which made me easy prey. Even though I put up a hard front with him that I would not accept certain things he could counter that with being extremely sweet. And the attention, time, and attitude he took with me worked. This melted me and blinded me at the same time as he would **play** the roll I was looking for *"The Knight in Shining Armor"* coming to my rescue in times of distress and easing my mind from certain worries. Not even a month had passed yet when he dropped the "this is how serious I am about you" conversation. I got some of a disclosure regarding his past and things he faced while I gave a full disclosure and we decided mutually to be together. Literally from that night he moved in with me and we were living together also another huge red flag but all I was seeing was that finally someone came who wanted to love me and be with me. So, I fell all in and gave him the benefit of the doubt including supporting us in the beginning. I was going to work, taking care of the bills, cooking, dealing with upkeep of the cottage, and helping him with his ventures. Now, I guess his conscience started to bite him in the butt because about two months after all this happened, he finally disclosed to me that he was still married to his wife with whom he was separated. Talk about a bomb to my chest but again I was already emotionally invested and blinded by the promise of the relationship. So, I gave him an ultimatum which included finalizing the divorce within 12 months and getting himself together to start pitching in budget wise by a deadline when I really should have thrown him out and let things be. But he agreed and moved forward with starting the divorce process and getting another job which made a total of two jobs in addition to the businesses he was trying to cultivate. So, I saw that as dedicated action. Little did I know! Eventually we got to the reason why his marriage started to fail, and it was because of living a double life having a wife on one island while having a mistress on another. This was another huge red flag but again I chose to believe he was a changing man with all the efforts he was putting forth. Until the day came that things started turning sour and he would use stupid excuses to start arguments with me and make me feel like I was just this horrible person who did not respect or listen to him. Looking back, I take full accountability for that because had I took the red flags seriously, I never would have gone through that. See, all women are born with intuition and when working correctly it tells you when something is wrong. I started seeing that there may have been another person in the mix just from his behavior. Blaming me for things, speaking to me disrespectfully, and one night even getting offended for me crying from the abuse. We managed to get in a semi good place when one day he went to a neighboring island on "Business", so I dropped him to the terminal, we said our goodbyes and I looked forward to his return after the weekend. However, on Sunday there was no communication, and he did not return. I did not get communication until Monday notifying me of his being jailed from being in an altercation with another person over money. While all this was happening, I was pregnant with no clue. So, I took the time from work, went to see what was going on and again it was like a bomb to my chest as I saw him imprisoned, seeming out of his mind, and from the reports the officers gave me they were under the same impression. I even went with him when the officers took him to the hospital to treat an injury he had. Now, I am in the middle of all this and beating myself up at the same time I return to life, went back to the toxic working environment only to discover not only was the man I loved in jail but that I would be having his child unmarried while he was still not divorced from his estranged wife. This relationship would be one of the hardest set of lessons I would learn for life. Moving forward I had to notify the company I worked for, pack up my life, move back in with my parents to conserve money, and prepare for bringing a new life into the world. This is where I think I checked out. I was here but not here which is extremely hard to explain. As a result, I went into my shell focused on taking care of myself, saving my money, doing my job, and planning. I also ended up making friends on the job which is something I was not supposed to do given past experiences. Later I would be reminded of why. So, given the situation I tried my best to be calm which I managed to do on the outside, but inside I was dying repeatedly, filled with sorrow, despair, rage, bitterness, and a low sense of worth. All while doing the doctor visits, working in the toxic place, and preparing my parents' home to house a newborn baby. I still tried to make things work and would repeatedly call Pretender long distance and make periodic visits to the jail where he eventually was placed for about one year.

While making all these preparations my sites once again turned to possibly moving to the states. This was also due in part to me wanting to ensure I was able to have my son in a place where everything was readily available, and I would not need to fly off island. So, I focused on seeking out a good doctor in Fort. Lauderdale. When the time came, I traveled to be seen before finally going up with my Mom and Dad to have my Son. We would be in Fort. Lauderdale for about a little over a month before I had my son. My Mother would also have surgery on both her eyes before and after my son's birth. While in Fort. Lauderdale, I took advantage of the Hospitals awesome programs for new moms to be. And would be asked questions prior to the birth that would be life changing. My son was born on December 8th, 2015, and though we had some scary moments he was perfect. At exactly 30 years old I now had these two bright eyes in my life looking to me. The focus became about him should something happen to me. Moments spent with him after his birth were filled with so many emotions that I could not really enjoy it. Now a single mom I had to somehow pull my life together, get a new game plan, and give him the best care possible. So, while taking on the new title of mom I bought as much things as I could on sale for him that would be needed and shipped them home, got his birth certificates, applied for his social security, and passport to make the journey back home. Once home the game plan then changed to finding a good doctor to monitor my son's growth, resume medical care for myself, and preparing my mind for going back to work while being a full-time mom. I got my will in place and covered all other financial responsibilities to make sure he would be taken care of in the event anything ever happened to me and vice versa.

Now, when I became a mother, something changed in me. I was always a perceptive person but there was a sense in me that became heightened. I was able to see things where I could not before, and this helped me in all the work that was going on with preparations and even with seeing the plots when I went back to work. Going back to work just two months after giving birth is not recommended. I was tired all the time, unable to eat well due to being tired and on top of that I had developed gall bladder stones that would give me horrific attacks. About four months after giving birth, I had to go out again to remove my gall bladder. This again was hard on me because now I could not lift anything, sit, stand, or lay for too long. In between all this I was still trying to visit my Sons Father in jail before and after the surgery making sure that he saw and could start forming a bond with his Son. During that time, I received a proposal for marriage that was accepted, thought things may be looking up, and maybe I just had to keep pushing. I was wrong there again because when a person shows you who they really are old habits die hard. When he came out of jail a few months after my surgery the plan was to start looking for a job depending on where he could complete probation, save, and move back when possible. We set a deadline; however, the deadline would come and go with no communication to me which introduced the time of little to no communication. I would not be given any physical addresses of where he lived, worked, and or any contact persons nearest to him in the event something happened. The excuse for the little to no communication would be, "I am working on building these businesses". So basically, I do not have time for you or my son. I was persistent however and whenever I could reach him would ask him what is going on and if there was not silence the answer would be "I Don't Know". After months of this behavior and me trying to get him to open up I just knew in my soul that something or someone else was taking his time and attention and that we were not a priority which started my process of disconnecting from him all together stopping any communication.

Then on September 7th, 2017, the US Virgin Islands was hit by Category 5 Hurricane Irma followed by Hurricane Maria just about one week later. There are no words that would ever put into explanation the devastation that I witnessed. Whole families were instantly homeless and relocated to the mainland US. As an essential worker I went into work along with many other co-workers who lost homes, belongings, cars, and we all did our part together with rebuilding. There were seven-day work weeks for months. We also got to meet some awesome folks who came down to help with the rebuilding from the US Mainland. This was a time whereas co-workers we became closer as people so friendships, alliances, associateships, and in some cases even situationships happened. It was at this moment that I met the next two great persons that would be of great significance in my life, and I will refer to them as "Guiding Light" and "The Catalyst".

Chapter 3 – The Awakening & Dark Night of the Soul

The Guiding Light and The Catalyst both came into the company shortly before the Hurricanes hit and because we were young and likeminded, I guess we all gravitated to each other to form what we called the A team comprised of "The Guiding Light", "The Catalyst", another co-worker in the office and myself. We made working fun, and got things done! After the Hurricanes we pulled ourselves together and leaned on each other when needing help on the work front. However, on the personal front The Catalyst made no stops in making sure I was known as the *"Work Wife"*. At first, I did not pay any attention but over a little time I came to really love him. Now here I was again, not even having time to heal and collect myself from the last one which resulted in having a child and becoming a single mother. But this time something else was happening and it was as if I was being drawn in like a moth to a flame. The Catalyst would give preference to only speak to me, setting me apart from the others in the office, and doing little things like sending messages through the other co-workers for me to call and do something for contact to be made. There would also be contact on breaks that would be overly sweet, and he would on occasion come into the office and make sure to visit me. We got so close I could even sense when I would get a call, and in work could almost finish each other's sentences. But this treatment would be sporadic with him at times disappearing with no contact then coming back and love bombing when I would become too quiet. At that time, I also started to feel some intense emotions. One night I even recalled having to leave my home and drive because I just felt like I was losing my mind, so I drove around the whole island screaming and crying. Things would be so up in the air with my life having just ended the last relationship to now feeling this way about someone else who could leave my life at any moment. Then, find out that this person was not single but acting like it. The whole thing became like an emotional roller coaster. Something that brought me so much joy had turned into a nightmare very quickly. Then I had to go home and be mommy. There was no time for me, no real attention to me, no real love for me, and I was going on empty giving so much of myself without filling myself up. In searching for some clarity of it all I spoke to my Guiding Light, and he gave me the best advise that I could not receive at the time saying, "you have to date around, don't put all your eggs in one basket", and "you should cut the friendship off with The Catalyst making things only professional". But would I listen? No! and things stayed that way until one day not too long before the end of my shift I got the word that "The Catalyst" was asking to speak with me and I knew it could not be anything about work. So, I took the call and received news that just broke my heart. I was told in a very immature way from "The Catalyst" that he was now Married! This moment marked the day that I started to wake up. As much as I grieved as if a loved one had literally died and sank into a deep personal depression just the same, I started seeking explanations for the things I was feeling, the intensity of the connection to this person, and what it meant. Just, as I started seeking answers to what I considered the shambles of my life people would be placed in my life that were gifted in senses beyond the sixth. Not only was I being guided in spirit but also in the physical realms. At this time because of the hustle and bustle I was not consistently involved fellowship wise in any religion. I was born into *"Christianity"* meaning my family on both sides were followers of Christ and as such were baptized and followed the teachings of *"Jesus Christ"* within the constructs of the Catholic Church. Because of the spiritual and physical state, I was in, that made me vulnerable to attacks and if you are faint of heart, I do not suggest you continue reading. The first person to advise me of the underlining energy affecting me said that someone was engaging in dark spiritual practices against me known as *"Dark Magic"* or better known in the Caribbean as *"Obeah"* and before I proceed, I know there will be a lot of people reading my account of what I have experienced and saying ok this lady is crazy. However, let me assure you I am with in my full 100% saine mind. I can give you many different reasons to believe what I say moving forward is true but unfortunately some experiences are not believable for many until they are experienced. This was one of the most difficult experiences I had going through *"Spiritual Warfare"* and *"Phycological Warfare"* which catapulted me into a *"Spiritual Awakening"*.

The first person that gave me information on what was happening was a friend of a friend of mine whom I connected with on a girl's night out. I was told several things regarding the heartbreak I was experiencing. Firstly, the woman that "The Catalyst" married went to a person in order accomplish several things. One was to blind the person to any other women so that he would only see her, the second was to get me out of their way accomplishing this goal in multiple ways that was not disclosed to me at that time. I was also informed that the reason I was experiencing so much strife where I worked was because there were people there connected to the same woman and they were collectively working in efforts to "get rid of me" or "get me out the way". I was advised there were two people who were filled with envy and hatred towards me proceeding with round table talks within their circle as to how this would be accomplished. This would later be shown to me in staged office situations and harassment I experienced from co-workers and the supervisor. The first action I was advised to take was not to eat from anyone where I worked and if I had to take anything accept it with my left hand and discard it in the garbage. The second action I was advised to take was to do a spiritual bath and pray for protection. The third action I was advised to take was to trust no one in the workplace. I was also given instruction on things I could do to help my situation, but it would involve magic work on people which I never have and never will subscribe too. I was also assured that for every bad transaction against me there would be a balanced counter action because of *"Divine Judgement"*, and I would be ok. Before connecting with the second gifted person, I would also go through nights of Hallucinations seeing shadows in my room and hearing what sounded like people shouting or shunning me which kept me up through most of the night (*similar to how Jesus may have experienced this on his route to the cross*). I would also experience on multiple occasions, while in bed, being awake preparing for sleep and feeling as if someone came onto my bed, laid next to me in a spooning position, and even hearing breath in my ear. On another occasion I was sleeping and woken out of my bed to see my hand slowly levitating as if someone was pulling my hand up.

After a period of years not remembering dreams, they became very vivid, memorable, and heart wrenching! Three particularly important dreams included first being visited by the outline of a black, void of color woman, with a halo type shape for a head, and spoke to me in the setting of a bedroom where I was laying down on a bed and seeing this figure in the doorway to the bedroom. At first, the room was dimly lit but as the voice spoke to me the light in the room became brighter, then a yellow\white snake slithered around my right arm until its head reached the inner part of my wrist, while I hear "it's the mother" (repeatedly) the snake bit into my wrist, and I awoke from feeling the pain of the bite while still feeling the fangs in my wrist once awake. The second dream again involved snakes and I remember being in a open field type setting with sporadic trees and seeing people around me as if sketched in black and white with snakes coiled around their arms as I had experienced but in the dream I remember myself and others trying to throw or get the snakes off. Then the field was covered with snakes, they hung from the trees, and people were positioned in different parts of the field (some standing, some laying half covered in snakes, some on bended knee) trying to get the snakes off and as I watched the scene intensify, woke up. The third dream consisted of being visited by an Angel. I did not know his name but knew where he was visiting me from. His face was round, was light brown in skin tone, and had features of an "African American". I was only allowed to see his face and he spoke to me assuring not to worry that "He will possess you". When the angel spoke these words, the understanding came, that this meant the assigned one who will walk with me in life was in the process of coming to me. Then, the Angel was gone, and the dream changed to a unfocused view of a man's hand holding a black box. The focus stayed on this view for some time slowly becoming clear as the hand with the box swayed, I heard the voice of a "Man" in a unclear conversation only making out the sounds as if plans were being carried out surrounding a boat.

For months I also developed symptoms of diarrhea, upset stomach, and lethargy. However, when I went to the Doctor and took tests to rule out what the issue was nothing was found out of the norm. I went through all these occurrences off and on for about a year all while dealing with heavy depression, working in a hostile workplace environment, caring for my son and parents, and trying to care for myself. One thing I can say is because of being blessed with the gift of attention to detail and foresight in the physical realm I have been able to dodge many bullets in personal and professional situations. With the affairs surrounding me there was no blueprint for me to follow and address all the different things happening to me much less how to recover from them. This was the time where my intuition kicked into overdrive and that still soft voice in me began to lead me in the areas I needed to go. I would get urges to google or seek information on the symptoms of what I was experiencing both in the relationship, with my health, in the workplace, and personally. The need to withdraw myself from people also became very apparent and even though it hurt me this included my son also at certain times. The only persons I could truly confide in were my parents and even with them I would not give full disclosure as to everything I was going through. So, I felt alone many times and yet even in those moments where I felt alone, I would get these urges to look for something like a topic, affirmations, go back into biblical scriptures, and even dive into phycological terminologies. It was at this time I started becoming acquainted with the traits of **Narcissism**, the different ways the abuse may look like from persons with this mental issue, and the effects it can have on people who are abused by it. I also became acquainted with the concepts of ***"Spiritual Awakening", "The Dark Night of the Soul", "Spiritual Journey", "Enlightenment", "Soul Contracts", "Soul Ties", Strong-Holds", "Energy", "Intention", "Karmic Cycles", "Karmic Partners", "Karma"*** and many other spiritual concepts that co-inside with what I was going through.

It was about four months after I connected with the first person that I met the second person. This time it was a Lady I connected with through social media all the way in Africa. Now, I passionately believe all these people were being spiritually guided to me because I would pray heavily during this time of my life, and one of the things I asked for was to know why. What was the cause of all this hatred and evil being sent to me through the mental, and spiritual intention of many people? Be careful what you put forward into this world with your intention and words because I received the answers. This time I would receive just about full disclosure because this Lady was able to feel what I went through breaking into tears and telling me exactly word for word what I experienced and even things to be aware of that were being attempted. This time, I was told that there was a woman who went to a spell caster in Haiti. For those of you who are not aware Haiti/Dominican Republic is one of the melting pots in the world where you will find people of this nature in addition to Dominica, Cuba, and Africa which are the areas closest to the part of the world where I live. This woman paid this spell caster to perform a ritual on "The Catalyst" and myself that would suppress his true feelings for me rendering him more controllable to her and amplifying my true feelings for him while keeping us separated. He was made to ingest something that made him vomit out his feelings for me aiding in the suppression of making any moves to leave her and move towards me. And this would be given to him occasionally which would make him have stomach or back issues every couple of months. In my case through eating occasions at work something would be placed in food items to keep me in the amplified state I was in which is why I could not cut off the friendship for so long and became stuck in waiting, being there for him, and giving my love/energy to him which would in turn be taken from him and given to her aiding in her keeping control over him. I was also told regarding me that I was supposed to be in a car accident as a result to kill me taking me out of her way and that she would not stop because of her hatred and need for vengeance. I went through the attempted vehicular crash that was influenced in spirit for me to go through and thanks to *Divine Intervention* came out without a scratch. The reason I was also going through so much strife in the workplace was also tied into an acquaintance of this person working where I was and the circle of women in the company connected to this woman who was doing all these things. The joist was to destroy me in all areas of my life, spiritually, mentally, emotionally, professionally, and eventually taking my life leaving my son motherless all-in order to accomplish using "The Catalyst" for her own purposes! After I received this information because of who I am the knot I felt in my stomach and the pain from reliving the trauma when this lady confirmed everything made me fall to my knees in tears then offer myself to my creator as his vessel for his great works. Could you ever imagine being faced with something even remotely like this and being attacked in just about every area of your life so much so that you cannot even see things clearly and live like this every day for years. This is a personal sacrifice! You are literally serving a life sentence in hell right here on earth. After that moment when I became aware of the full scope of what people are truly capable of, I thought about my "Granny" my Fathers Mother. The memories I have of my Granny are not many but what I do remember was that she was kind, gave me cookies and milk when I came to visit, and allowed me to watch tv if I did all my homework. What stuck with me about my Granny was how strong of a woman she was. My Granny gave birth to nine children and raised them all including burying one at six months old while running businesses out of her home. My Granny was an amazing force! I still here her words of wisdom through my Father in stories of her acts of kindness, fairness, and no-nonsense teachable moments. While capable of sweetness my Granny learned to have a good balance especially in the arena of upholding respect for herself with others and remembering her would remind me of the stock I came from. My Granny is one of the most influential women in my life which would also later be affirmed after all the tests and trials I went through in my career. The more time passed while in my reclusively I also thought about my Mama and her humble strength, my Mother and her discrete rebellion watching her in her life battles, my Aunt Marilyn and her dedication to make an impactful difference in the community. These women were the stock I came from and were the living embodiments of the legacy I was a part of. So, despite the opposition against me I would continue to hold my own; gain the strength to keep my game face on, do my best pulling myself together while healing from past traumas, identify and change damaging mindsets accumulated over the years, learn to protect myself and my energy from outside influences, nurture and provide myself with love while opening myself to the greatest love ever known, invested in myself through seeking knowledge on an array of different topics, set clear boundaries with people/the institution I worked in, and created plans in private with divine guidance. Because of how social I became after the storms I had to revert to my introverted tendencies from my early school days and do research every moment I could get time. In the past I developed a love of crystals/minerals and their benefits so when I learned about grounding, I used this work in helping me to protect, heal, and ground myself. The concept of working with crystals/minerals is quite simple. Crystals/Minerals are not only geological. If you research how they are formed, you will understand that they grow over time. So, as we grow over time so do, they. The benefit of collecting them is *energy*. Crystals/Minerals hold energy and are good natural tools that connect you with nature which is good for grounding and connecting with yourself. Working with them also helps to get you into good routines or practices. Exercising proper maintenance of cleansing and reprograming your crystals/minerals can introduce you to the principals of having a good spiritual practice. The different methods of cleansing them are remarkably like the practices of cleansing our own energy. Salt water or sea water can purge old energy, so can burying them in the earth which is also where most crystals/minerals grow, and lastly using the cleansing smoke from sage – a herb known for its energy cleansing properties. With us the same principals apply with intention we can purge negative or toxic energy from our bodies, use grounding techniques like walking bare foot on the grass or bare ground/sand, and we can also use the cleansing properties of sage to purge negative energy from ourselves and personal spaces. Each type of crystal is known for their energy attributes. For example, hematite carries strong energy of grounding so much so (if you are in tune) you can feel it as you hold it. This mineral is good for sharpening your concentration, memory, will power, confidence, and aids in forming an energetic protective barrier prohibiting the absorption of negativity from others, and overcoming addictions. When kept within your vicinity or worn on the body this mineral energetically aids in the regulation of anemia, supports the kidneys, tissue regeneration, aids in the proper absorbing of iron, directly treats the issues of insomnia as well as anxiety, and can also aid in the healing of bone fractures and the alignment of the spine – scoliosis. Crystals/Minerals can also hold and amplify your energetic intentions, or you can think of this as a programmer to a computer. After cleansing you would hold your crystal and concentrate or think of what your intention is for as long as you like. You can do this repeatedly while meditating, keep a regular routine of touching your crystal/mineral, and keep a regular routine of cleansing/re-programing your crystals/minerals. Becoming aware of the beneficial attributes for each crystal/mineral tells you the best one you would want to work with intentionally. Crystals/Minerals are also used in many different religions for example Japamala or mala prayer beads can be comprised of different crystals shaped and polished to create beads used in forming a necklace type prayer tool used in Buddhism, Hinduism, Jainism, and Sikhism. Each bead would represent a prayer in a succession of prayers also like the rosary in Catholicism which can also be comprised of crystal/mineral beads. Personally, I have come to think of crystals/minerals as companions that assist in my healing/deepening my connection to myself and ultimately the Creator.

The beginning of my healing process started with re-engaging my crystal/mineral work, withdrawing myself from other people socially and in communication, spending more time with myself in *silence / prayer / meditation / research / self-care / self-love / rest*. I began to invest more of my time and energy into myself and deepening connection with the Creator. I reviewed past journals and started keeping a current one to document feelings, findings, and later prophetic information. The consistency of the changes I made started to slowly change my situation and perception. The harassment attempts in my job became more spread apart as I would thoroughly document dates, times, and situations as they occurred, reported through the chain of command/human resources/the necessary government agencies, and followed due process regarding the issues experienced. One of the things I asked for in prayer was a strong spirit of *discernment*, and *heightened intuition* to be able to *see people and situations as they truly are*. As time progressed people's true nature and secret plans were revealed. I would respond by *cutting any communication* past the company work and started separating myself from being in the office as much as possible taking my break times, leaving the building, drinking more teas, and connecting with the Creator in the silence outside of the workplace. Even while working I would recite *prayers, affirmations,* and later *declarations* over my life *(The Law of Decree)* and all *The Universal Laws of Higher Frequency!*

These changes also brought about the introduction of the third set of people sent to me which was a team of two Ladies out of Florida who were able to give me the final piece of the puzzle which would lead me to asking the right questions and receive the right answers. I was told that there was heightened spiritual protection around me and that there was so much opposition at the workplace because I was not supposed to be there. When you are not in the right place in your life and there is a divine purpose for you there will also be opposition that urges you to make necessary changes leading onto the right path of fulfilling your purpose. Often to many times we fall into *comfort zones* and my comfort was my work. I loved what I did in my profession, and this kept me in that company way longer than I should have been. However, the opposition would gradually intensify to assist in moving me to where I needed to be. In my case the opposition called out all the stops using *lies, manipulation, gossip, intimidation, harassment, nepotism,* and *micromanaging*. It also became apparent that the person I was reporting to in human resources was also covering for the supervisor as the responses to my complaints on harassment would only be responses reiterated from the supervisor's initial response.

In the months leading to the moment everything would come to a head I also started noticing *signs and synchronicities* either in *time sequences, numbers in my work, videos I would watch on youtube, and even in the events occurring via changes in department processes as well as with the management members companywide either quitting, being promoted, or the company's infrastructure being changed to accommodate downsizing*. The number sequences really gained my attention, and I would investigate what they might mean such as *333, 1111, or 555*, and I came to understand that this was the method of which my *heavenly team was communicating*, showing their support, and providing guidance. One of the things I asked for in prayer was to let an open channel to heavenly guidance be established which I received. This was the establishment of me realizing my worth. *Heaven was showing me you are loved, you are supported, and you are protected. It is ok to proceed with confidence!* However, I would also be told when I needed to work on something. This led to me being told what the divine plan was for me. Because of this, I started to receive large amounts of information over a period of two months. Some may call this receiving prophetic words. I was told that I would be laid off and, in the months, leading to the layoff I would be involved in a series of tests that I would have to stand my ground on which also happened. I also received names of whom was trying to get information from me to provide for this inner circle in the company wanting to keep close tabs of my activities. Through changes in perception, I also came to a bigger understanding of what is currently happening not just in my surroundings but in the world. There was a shift in power taking place. People like me, a person who felt *unworthy*, and the *least likely* would be placed in *positions of authority*. This deeper understanding was a revelation putting everything that happened to me over the course of my life into *perspective*. The more time I dedicated to communing with my heavenly team the more I no longer sought validation from the world. *Silence became my weapon*, and I would be still in moments of peace and communication with my creator. This led to me being a lot calmer in situations as they came. A confidence was exuded in me so much that I no longer fed into the *illusions* this world places in front of us like there will be no good change, you will not be victorious, you will be held in bondage, you will be subjected to orders of man, and you have no power. Yet here I was, one woman, summoning the convergence of people holding meetings to discuss the threat I was, how to get rid of me, and executing plots to accomplish that in addition to summoning principalities to accomplish their goal for me. No longer did I worry about if I lost my job because I was assured of support in the **highest place**. In the months leading to the series of events ending with my being laid off I started to receive creative ideas on becoming an entrepreneur. Part of my research was on creating my own businesses, financial investment/insurance, phycological conditions and tendencies people carry respective to them, spiritual concepts, learning my rights in this country/resources available in your defense, and finally principals of self-care and love. From diving into all this knowledge and wisdom and as a part of my healing process I created my first business conveniently titled "The Journey to Self" which is a blog on facebook that I turned into a platform for people like myself that maybe just be finding themselves going through "Awakening". In my blog I would post online articles on experiences or concepts others have discovered or were speaking on in addition to my own experiences with certain spiritual concepts and resources on my journey. The blog would also be used as a tool to empower small business owners following their passions and providing their services to the community through free advertisements posted. I would also post information on positive tools that could be used by the community such as free or affordable educational events, government announcements, positive press information about our tourism-based economy, works of great authors throughout history, and a ton of reading material for self-help, healing, and development. Never in my wildest dreams would I imagine this one creation would become an **Enterprise**. More development ideas came to me for the expansion of the blog, and so did the ideas for many other businesses. I was assured that I have all the resources needed or it would be sent to me and started working on the website platform for my blog which would expand to advertisement, merchandise, and appointments for life coaching sessions once certified. I started to research the right institution to gain certification adding to the knowledge I already gained and acquired it. Then, the idea of becoming an author based on my journey was born. The cord was cut on tv. Youtube became the place where a lot of time was spent listening to content creators on their channels describing their journeys and it dawned on me that the platform, I created with my blog is needed. There are no set blueprints to follow as everyone's journey is different. However, the tools and principals I came across could be used to help based on each individual journey. No longer did I feel alone! There were so many similar situations I heard about, life coaches I found speaking about the different tactics of abuse Narcissists use across many different environments, and enlightened persons now sharing their own personal ministry's. Slowly I started to find my tribe through like-minded persons who are awakened and following in the ordered footsteps before them through social media, youtube, and many other digital platforms to get their messages out globally. I even had the pleasure of arranging collaborations for working with youtubers on future projects. Local businesses were reaching out to me requesting to be liked by my blog and the opportunities just kept coming.

Chapter 4 – Walking in my Purpose

         January of 2020, I watched from my cubicle desk as the World learned about the devastative loss of life in China because of the *Covid 19 Virus*. Not only were the numbers in the thousands but the virus quickly spread to different countries across Europe eventually making its way to the United States within the span of about two weeks which also resulted in thousands of lives lost very quicky in addition to a progressive lock down of many countries across the globe. Even where I was on a tiny Island in the Caribbean the virus made its way which sparked several lock downs over time. As an essential worker I worked and watched as many other essential workers went into work losing their lives in service to the masses. Many companies went belly up, millions of people lost their jobs, became confined to their homes, international travel for many countries stopped completely or became limited to essential flyers such as diplomats or corperate representatives with private conglomerates. The world as we know it changed in what seemed like the blink of an eye.

         I also witnessed the massive shift from our physical way of living to a more remote way of living. Business, meetings, and gatherings were conducted over the internet using platforms such as Zoom, Facebook, Google, and many other web platforms or apps. School children transitioned to at home distance learning using many of the same platforms. And literally as if overnight new virtual businesses were being created and heavily advertised online as well as new products and services that were introduced to accommodate the new normal of social distancing (as if it was all planned). Restaurants diversified themselves to pick up service through apps, websites, or call-in ordering. On the island I live the government also transitioned many public services to remote servicing as well. Registering your car, applying for a business license, and many other services became accessible to the public through online applications or methods of remote servicing through the mail, fax, or email. It was after this period of drastic upheaval that I identified the need for me to start working on my business projects. I never really felt that I fit in working for businesses, or under other people. So, I started doing the research on different business ideas, costs, elements for incorporation, registering for a business license, and all other aspects revolving around creating a business. I also started journaling on information I found or ideas I had to use as points of reference. The work that I was doing was investing in myself and that led me on a path of not being aligned as a worker in the position I held. I would not agree with many of the policies or procedures that either existed and needed updating or were new and coming down the pipeline. This led to a lot of conflict in the position I held because I was no longer thinking as a good soldier who just does as they are told but as a general strategizing, being the voice behind much needed change, and militantly standing up for fare treatment. With the change in mindsets, I also started separating myself from being so wrapped up with my energy and time placed in my career.

Outside of my career, home life, and personal life I became more discerning with dating by putting up my boundaries, standing my ground, paying attention to red flags, and walking away if a situation was not honoring me. I made that list of what a partner looks like for me based on what is **_GOOD_** for me and not what may be or had potential. Because I was also employed full-time and engaged in a lot of self-love\development while nurturing a young son this did not leave much time for me to go out and physically meet new people especially with the heightened security and personal health protective measures in place. So, I used what I knew about the most which was the internet. It was time to start making the effort and making new acquaintances! The dating part of my facebook account was activated, and I built my profile to connect with single men that held the same or similar standards as I was looking for in a partner. Through this platform I would go through many profiles and spoke with a few of the gentlemen, but the conversations would not lead anywhere. The fact that most guys were using this platform to meet ladies for convenience was very apparent! This also became apparent in some of the other dating sites making my efforts to find a good connection extremely difficult. However, I would not be detoured from the disappointments and just as I kept going with everything else in my life continued to keep putting myself out there using the best options possible. Then, about three months later, out of nowhere as I was looking through the new set of suggested profiles on facebook dating there he was. His picture stood out, it was full body, he was dressed in a formal suit, his posture was confident and with his facial expression there was a slight smile, but in his eyes, there was just something I could not explain that connected with me. That still soft voice urged me to initiate contact which I did. Recognizing that this profile was different there was no fear of will he reach out, will he like me, will this go anywhere, and all the other self-sabotaging chatter in my mind was just not there. The feeling as though everything will be ok was there and this allowed me to just move on, continue in my own self-work, and day to day activities. *I was learning to just let things be without worrying about my being able to control the outcome and applying practical application of that naturally*. Just a few days after sending the like notification I received a match from him, and he reached out telling me that he loved my pictures and profile.

Now, after communication was established the urge for me to investigate a little more about him became overwhelming. We are all aware that people use the internet for many devious purposes so just to ensure that the picture was the actual person I did a little mild background check. What I saw and was able to legally verify through public records was commendable. His first profession was like that of my Dad and right away this established deeper insight into his principals and life choice in public service. Anyone who knows me for most of my life will be able to tell you that I share a special connection with my Father, and I have been blessed to have him in my life consistently since my birth. My father was there through just about every milestone in my life, has been my confidant, rock in times of trouble, protector, provider, and one of my biggest supporters so as a result you would see me mostly out with my Dad even now. After the check this made me a little more encouraged and instead of worrying about if this man is everything negative in the book chose to stay in the positive energy of who he was showing himself to be based on his life choices. Conversation at first covered the typical pleasantries like "good morning", "how are you", and "what are you doing", and after about three weeks some of our personalities would show as we progressed to facetiming. The difference this time around was also speaking with at least two other gentlemen so my *energy* was not completely focused on one person which is what I would normally do when I met someone that I really connected with. This allowed me to **not chase** because my time was literally stretched between everything, so I naturally fell into a position of **letting them come to or contact me** with the occasional check in on my part. The other plus was that two of the gentlemen were off island, so this allowed me to take my time and establish getting to know them well before meeting anyone. I wanted to be well acquainted with everyone and be able to determine who held the same to similar standards as what I was looking for in a partner and who was just looking for a fling. Taking my time would be the best thing ever because only one out of the three would express wanting the same things in a relationship as I was looking for. Also, only one gentleman was having the conversations about meeting while the others were just ok with conversing. The one who was really showing me that he was interested in a long-term relationship and possibly more along with being eager to meet me was my guy that I reached out to.

One day noticing I had some possible time off from work I reached out to my guy, asked what he would be up to for the weekend, and the response was eagerly I am available, so I confirmed that I was too. What I loved was that he **took charge** of the conversation once I hinted that some time was coming up and offered to take care of me as a treat in coming over to meet (this was something I never experienced before). This offer also came after I had turned him down a few times regarding meeting. So even though I was a little apprehensive I agreed to accept his offer but only under the condition that it was for the day. Now, up until this point I did not have any self-sabotaging conversations in my mind. However, the morning I woke up to go meet him I became so nervous on the way to the airport thinking what if he did not like me, what if he is a jerk, and all the other thoughts that all pointed to me not really thinking I was enough for this Man or that he was not enough for me started flooding my thoughts. Then I caught myself being triggered by my nervousness and stopped, took deep breaths, and spoke life into my situation affirming to myself that I was more than enough and that it made no sense worrying. I was going to find out and get to the point confirming if this Man liked me or did not then just keep it moving. Even though I was still extremely nervous about the first meeting with affirming myself I was able to calm down, get into beast mode, and place my confidence to the forefront. As nervous as I may have been, I tucked it deep down inside myself and focused on breathing and grounding while I waited on the flight. On the twenty-minute flight over to the island where he lived the sky was clear, the clouds were white, the ocean a deep blue and I focused my energy on being grateful to whiteness so much beauty on the way to see him. Thankfully, the flight over was so peaceful that when I arrived was feeling good, sat down outside the arrival terminal, and as I proceeded to reach for my phone letting him know I was there he called me first and led me just a few short steps away from where I was sitting as he had been there for some time waiting for me to arrive. This made me smile inside knowing that he made it a *priority to be early*. As, I walked up to his car, he opened his door with a smile, greeted me with a hug and opened the door for me to get in the car. There was nothing set in stone other than to walk with beach ware as he had suggested maybe going jet skiing, to the beach, or pool. And because there were no set plans, I was just up for whatever adventure naturally happened. While on the ride from the airport I could not help but discretely glimpse over at him as he was driving, and he was even more handsome than his pictures. I also had not been to the island for a while so I would also gaze out at the scenery once I noticed him glimpsing over at me. I felt peaceful in his presence and before I knew it, we pulled into a very well-known hotel on the island and entered a gated private neighborhood. As he pulled into his driveway, and we came out of the car there were a set of stairs descending to the home. He did something that I rarely saw other than from my Father and that was offer his hand to give me *support* walking down the stairs! Just from his manors I was already impressed but maintained composure. Walking into his home felt like I went away on a trip to Fiji and had my own private Villa. His home felt warm, cozy, and most importantly peaceful. In my mind after so many years of turbulence in my life I thought, ***God is this how much you love me!*** It was difficult for me to hold back the tears, but I maintained and gave my thanks in private! After making me feel very welcomed and settling myself he led me to the kitchen offering breakfast if I had not eaten yet which I graciously accepted, and he sprang into action declining any assistance when I tried to offer. So, I graciously backed down and watched this man cook breakfast while introducing me to a healthier way of preparing bacon. As we ate, we talked getting a feel for each other, and starting the real getting to know you process. The day for me was like a dream! I can still remember the feeling of the energy, so peaceful! From where I was seated there was a view of the beach and the ocean, you could see the birds flying, hear the faint crashing of the ocean on the beach, and feel the cool breeze. With every interaction I was treated respectfully so much that it even felt regal. He was ***attentive*** making sure I had everything needed and more. After breakfast we retired to the living area where we would innocently fall asleep on each other upon the couch. Being so tired from the hustle and bustle of the week after we woke up, I fell back asleep, and he was so understanding that I was left in peace to rest. When I finally woke up, I felt good, rested, at peace, and finally right where I belonged! Unfortunately, it was also time for him to make sure I got back to the airport in time for the flight back home. Six hours went by in the blink of an eye and on the way to the airport he introduced me to one of his co-workers as well as trying to include me in a family conversation over the phone. He was showing me I want you in my life in so many ways. I even recall him asking "can you stay forever". I hate to say it but because I had been through so many unworthy relationships in the past where I was the one carrying mostly everything, going through that experience had me shocked, and almost in disbelief that *finally* here is someone willing to *reciprocate*! Almost arriving to the airport, I felt myself become saddened that the time with him came to an end and looking forward to what was going to happen next. He also became incredibly quiet as I did just before we got to the airport. When we arrived at the departure terminal, he got out of the car and embraced me with a hug that I turned "church appropriate" and as I walked away from him, he blew me kisses before driving off as I got to the counter. It all happened in a Blur, so fast! I had so many emotions flowing through me but when I got into the terminal to wait for my flight, sat down, and settled myself. I recall looking through the glass wall past the airport runway to the hills that surrounded the airport, how the rays of the sun fell to the ground, the clouds seemed to be spread out perfectly in the sky as evening was approaching. This scene was almost as if the Angels in Heaven were telling me everything is going to be ok. Then, I started to reflect on how many times this happened on my way over, while I was at his home, and finally in the departure terminal as I waited for my flight back home. Three times I saw and felt peace in nature during the entire trip also an incredibly significant number! As I sat in the beauty of the peacefulness in the scenery there came the butterflies in my stomach while I got lost in r&b until it was time to leave.

Going back home to the hustle and bustle kind of made me a little sad but I got back into a grove to keep going. After that day communication became sparse from him with only about two messages asking how I was doing and the last saying there was much more to come before *radio silence!* I reached out many times with growing concern for about two weeks to then come to the realization that I just need to let things be. Of course, this was another blow! But instead of presuming all sorts of scenarios I stopped, prayed, and meditated on the situation. Finally, I concluded that there is no direct answer to what happened, and my faith was being tested so while I was still concerned continued letting things be until the answer presented itself. I also would conduct research on this behavior as I am a person that seeks answers. In my research I would become enlightened with many psychological terms and current concepts that would not only open my eyes to the possibilities of this situation but with many others in my life. What I experienced was a concept called *Ghosting* in a *Runner/Chaser* dynamic. When you are ghosted this is a period where the other person just cuts all communication with you. This is also a tactic commonly used by *Narcissists*. In my study of *Narcissism,* I learned that while there are people who suffer completely from this mental disorder there are just some people who exhibit some traits and tendencies which can fall back on a person's upbringing/family dynamics. There are also different types of Narcissists. In this research I also found out about the perfect relationship that is sought out by Narcissists. This introduced me to their Spiritual and Psychological paring with *Empaths* and the *Super Empaths* or extremely sensitive people. Learning about the traits and characteristics of these types of people shocked me as I noticed carrying a lot of those traits. Physically this explained why so many ass holes were attracted to me and why I took positions of being understanding, over giving, chasing, giving too many chances, trying to save everyone at the expense of myself, and staying too long in situations not serving to me that became abusive. The same basic principles applied with Empaths that they are one hundred percent Empathic or only have certain traits which again falls back on a person's upbringing/family dynamic. Just as Narcissistic persons suffer from unaddressed childhood trauma so do Empaths and they are opposites on the same spectrum. Literally light and dark seeking out each other. If I did not meet this man, I would not have gone down the rabbit hole of doing the research to ultimately find out more about who I am. And in that research also learned to protect myself against the traps and tactics used by Narcissists to keep Empaths under their control serving as the best suppliers for their Egos. I learned to no longer ignore red flag behavior and not give so many chances to people. I learned to have people prove themselves to me instead of proving myself. This information lit up just about every area of my life and gave me more of an understanding as to why I was caught in repetitive cycles. While I in no way think that my guy is a complete Narcissist, I got an understanding into what may have happened with him. Most importantly after experiencing so much rejection I learned that it truly can be Gods protection and just as I was learning about myself maybe he was too. Also, I could not ignore how good I felt when I was with him which I took as a peek into what could be in store if I continue investing in, refining, educating, and making the best decisions for my life with divine guidance. I was still also receiving downloads that things would only be ghosted for a time and learned the art of letting go with love and light instead of chasing to fix things believing I am the problem. Now armed with this new knowledge I continued researching about Narcissists and applying practical application to protect myself. **Ghosting, Gaslighting, Manipulation, the art of Deception, Energy, Intention, Flightiness, Love-Bombing, Fast Actions, Strategy**, and all the different tools of the trade for Narcissistic persons became a focus for me. This even brought people who were on the same journey as myself into my life who were seeking clarity on the same behavior. As for being Empathic this brought to light making peace within myself by forgiving all the decisions, beliefs, and mindsets that caused me so much trauma and pain throughout my life. My value shined brighter than the stars as I began changing into a new person, gaining knowledge, honoring myself, learning the importance of saying **No**, **walking away**, and not having to do anything extra to **prove myself by just being myself**. The mindset of being a drop in the bucket changed. This gave me more **self confidence** and **trust** in the knowledge that **I am worthy of love and was made perfectly**. Just as I learned the tools of the trade for Narcissists, I also learned the tools of the trade for Empaths which disclosed the **spiritual gifts** that I could not place an identity to.

While in this waiting period a whirlwind of changes would occur. Firstly, I would again have to be focused on standing my ground and following due process about being targeted in the office, going back and forth in meetings, documenting, and presenting my case multiple times while being thrown into orchestrated fear and intimidating situations of harassment with certain persons making false accusations on me to management, and concocted harassment investigations from the parties involved with the supervisor against those not subscribing to the secret life of their circles activities. This also happened while I started realizing that Angelic guidance was reaching out to me in the form of number sequences. I identified their meanings which presented messages pertaining to what I was going through, what I needed to do, where to go, and what I needed to work on moving through the obstacles being thrown at me. During this time, I recognized being seen in the physical\spiritual realms and the **reason why**. My position was not assimilating into toxicity\darkness\being under control and I was moving on the side of **light**, **choosing to honor myself** and in doing so **honored my Creator**.

Also, in seeking my creator by **praying, meditating, moving in my truth, and then at that point being obedient in following the guidance being given to me I was following the path to my purpose being revealed to me just as it was orchestrated**. I was showing that

I acknowledged my wrongs, learned my lessons, and was choosing to be **obedient** instead of trying to **control everything** this action invited my Creator into **every aspect of life**. My perception changed from choosing everything in my life to communing with my Creator and running it by **divine guidance** before **moving**. When this change happened, it took away the need to seek validation from anyone else and this was <u>**KEY**</u>. When I looked to my Creator for advice, love, validation, vindication, justice, and fulfillment through purpose everything in my life **started to change**! The stagnancy slowly went away! The players were being moved to accelerate things coming to a head where I worked. First, the supervisors boss suddenly up and quit, then all the chaos came which led to me standing my ground again until it was decided that the best way to **get rid of me** was to use the upcoming "Layoffs" and this was a joint effort through different circles in the company. Now, what they did not know or maybe even did not care about was the fact that in every meeting held, plan organized, and times of follow through they were being seen and before anything came to pass, I would receive what I like to call downloads from divine guidance informing me of what was to happen and how to proceed. Two months before the layoff I was made aware of this process to take place and as I received instruction would proceed accordingly understanding that this was what I signed up for!

See, there is a concept I learned about called a **DIVINE PLAN**. For some, before we are born into this world, we agree in the form of a contract to follow through with a specific divine plan for our lives here on earth. And all this information is kept in sort of a heavenly library better known as what you may hear some people referring to as the **Akashic Records** or **Amenti Hall**! The physical receives influence on its structure from somewhere and that somewhere is the **Spiritual Realm**. So, most concepts such as contracts, record keeping, and even places where records are kept come from the realm of the **Spirit**. Now, slowly over this two-month period not only was I advised on what to do regarding the chaos at work, but on what I was before my existence on earth, who I am now, and what I was divinely destined for was revealed. My guy who just went radio silent was revealed to have a significant role in my life and was still being prepared for what was to come as I was. I was assured that it would take some time, but he would contact me, that we together have a mission to accomplish, how that would leave a lasting positive impact on our community, and the changes to come from our efforts that would leave a legacy blessing not only our lineage but our Community as well! Processing all of this was at times **hard** in the beginning, I questioned my **sanity**, but just to confirm that I was not crazy not too long after getting a download I would see what I was informed of **come to pass**. When you open yourself to the greater good beyond yourself, the Creator, Universe, or whatever name you have for our Source can **blow your mind!** What you can conceive is limited vs. what the vision is from the Creator for us. The level to which I was shown rising too was **mind blowing!** Even now I stop and think **Father\Mother you love me this much!** However, all the positive changes also depended on my ability to **obey with the spiritual guidance being provided to me**. I had reached a level in life that showed me the way of the world was discarding me, opposing me, and slowly over time leading me to an **early grave just to repeat the same cycles in the next life**. Now, armed with the knowledge of the divine plan for me just as David was armed with the plan for his destiny to be a King. I made a conscious decision to walk in the footsteps being ordered before me, learned the art of **SELF MASTERY, and started to expand by initiation into Christ\Sophia (Christos-Sophia) Consciousness….**

Chapter 5 – Being Still

The obstacles I passed gave me the encouragement to continue complying with divine instruction, the dust started to settle as I received the layoff notice and faced the many different jabs that were meant to get me acting out of character and distracted from evolving past what ***they were showing me my value was***. Behind closed doors, many persons I worked with sought to ***destroy my reputation*** preventing any form of promotion in that environment as well. The more this happened, the more I proved their words wrong by not engaging in their traps and completing my time there ***working to the absolute best of my ability until the last day*** while reporting any harassing situations with due process. In continuing the ordered course placed before me this included learning to ***be private*** by cutting all communication to everyone at work and once this was done those in the secret circles showed who they were even more. Unfortunately, this would mean I would have to distance myself even from associates I formed strong relationships with which was a struggle, and this was also one of my lessons in discovering as much as you think someone may be for you when in an environment as this one no one can be trusted. Concerns were brought to my attention from certain parties regarding "what I was going to do", and "if I wasn't afraid of financial hardships" in attempts to learn my business and put me in a state of fear and supplication. Yes, there were people sent to me in the guise of being concerned about my wellbeing when the true intention was to find out my next steps to inform others who feared me enough to take certain steps within the company and outside the company in efforts to suppress me from rising in position and social status. Who I am and what I represented was ***a threat!*** I was the person who identified issues and resolution for them. I brought *light* and *attention* to things that people did not want to have changed because **problems served their agendas** (This is a tactic used in many other areas of life not just in workspaces). In any environment this type of person is a threat. The comfort zone of many can be changed as a result. And not only was I doing this, but others were watching who agreed and started to follow suit. I was the person who stood for equality and fairness in the workplace in addition to being a person who brought about *changes* in the way business was conducted for quality and that was contagiously spreading. Pride was taken in the way I spoke with clients, co-workers, and in the work I produced. This placed a spotlight on others that took a backseat to the position they were given making me even more of a threat.

In the days that led up to my last at that company initially I was in my feelings about all the time I invested but eventually I was calmed by getting the downloads of full disclosure regarding why I was being moved from the environment I was in. Clearly, I was able to see the toxicity in the mindsets, policies, and poor leadership that kept me distracted from investing in myself and what I was meant to do for years because I was putting so much of my time, energy, and talent into the position I held. To heal I could not remain working there. While at the same time I saw why I was placed there because it was in that place, I would receive the lessons, preparation, and education for where I am being led to next on my Journey. In private I healed from the trauma of the betrayals and was even grateful to my transgressors for being educators in the art of deception, manipulation, mindfulness, self-respect, and determination which all sharpened my discernment abilities. Spread over the course of about nine years I gained valuable knowledge preparing me for greater levels of everything I have gone through because of the ascension I am going through based on the confirmed levels I will rise to in life. When the time came, I chose to accept my destiny, followed my divine purpose, and became a **_LIGHTWORKER_**. Now, there are many different definitions of what a lightworker is and does. However, in the heavy research of myself, my qualities, and with divine guidance it was made known to me that light working is a large part of my purpose. My understanding of light working is also being a person who engages in **_good works_** that positively impacts, inspires, influences, and or acts as catalysts to changing the world positively, raising the vibration of the planet, and **_leading by the example of doing their own self-work_** providing priceless wisdom for others and lighting the path through the darkness in this life. So, after going through unacceptable treatment with poor communication for what I needed to do exiting the company these were the thoughts that filled my head giving me a good feeling while transitioning from a worker to an **_Enterprise Creator._**

The first two weeks I could clearly see how working in that place **_drained me_** because what I mostly did was catch up on much needed rest. In between a two-week period, I would continue to receive more jabs from the company in the form of ridiculous insurance amounts to pay while being unemployed, and still not receiving any documentation on my harassment complaint prior to lay off. Again, I ignored the jabs and once getting the rest I needed was able to regroup getting things together that I now needed to put in place for myself and my Son. My energy levels started to go up and I started working on creating my business projects that were put down due to my career. I started investing in myself through taking online courses in preparation for launching my first business in addition to growing my social media following. And, just as I was promised by divine guidance, everything I could have possibly needed was provided for me. My home office was finally arranged, all the paperwork that co-insides with lay off was completed, and I was able to focus on organizing my projects. This book is the second project from which many other projects are in the making and all *divinely inspired*!

Continuing in my personal work would bring additional revelations regarding issues I still held inside myself. The practice of **LETTING GO** kept being brought to my attention by divine guidance. Though I felt as if I had made peace with what happened to me, I was still holding onto some of the pain and the trauma from certain experiences throughout my life. As I re-lived the accounts of experiences while writing this book there were times, I still found myself engulfed in tears. So, I understood what I was being told to do and during this time of being accountable for my own time not having to punch a clock I started the inner work of forgiving myself, speaking life into myself, healing, and working on my faith in the prophetic promises given to me by divine guidance. By the third week I formed my own routine that involved a healthy balance of investing my time between taking care of my Son, working on my personal development, and business projects. I was also being given lots of encouragement in the work I was doing with my blog so much so that other projects came forth from it such as a Women's Empowerment Conference. I was graciously honored by being asked to attend as a guest speaker. Encouragement from my guidance team also pointed out to me something that I had struggled with most of my life since that crushing moment of being that young girl watching her boyfriend in the infamous kiss that changed the perception of myself. Finally, I had to confront my issues with my value and being vulnerable. Moving forward in my life holding on to these debilitating mindsets of how I saw myself, and repetitive thinking of the pain from the trauma I have been through would only serve as new blocks in my ascension. While going through the process of writing this book on many occasions the thoughts of will my work really make an impact, the world only looks at a credible source for wisdom and am I good enough to bring forth my experiences and knowledge for the benefit of others. So, I focused on how I could work on these issues finally addressing them and letting them go to make room in my life for new mindsets that would serve my ascension into promises assured to me by divine guidance. In this time of waiting I faced, felt, and moved through emotions, trauma, and self-image issues in multiple ways. The first was addressing my eating habits and overall health. The second was paying attention to what I was feeding my mind and spirit changing the type of content I viewed, read, or listened to ensuring the consumption of mostly self impowering information, or reflections of true love such as taking up a hobby watching inter-racial family's way of living through vlogs and social media platforms while supporting them and sharing their channels through my platforms. Time was now more available to dedicate to communing with my creator in prayer, meditation, and in word. The things I needed to do were made noticeably clear to me and as they were pointed out I would go into action addressing them as best as I could through the principles of affirmation, self-care/love, prayer, meditation, declaration, forgiveness, letting go, being still, and self-development. I also investigated the spiritual and health benefits of fasting while practicing the other principals and slowly I saw my perceptions change. Just one month into not punching a clock my mind was made up to continue investing in myself and using the natural talents and wisdom given to me in service to others through my own coaching practice and writings. While I still was putting myself out there professionally another sign that was showing me, I made the right decision was not getting any responses and or receiving notices that while I had good credentials other candidates were being chosen over myself or would not compensate me for my value. So, most of my time and energy remained poured into my son, self, project developments, and most importantly deepening my connection to the *Creator*.

This was a time of deep reflection, soul searching, purging, healing and recognition. I began to have revelation after revelation regarding why certain things had to happen. It was for me to graduate to the next phase of life prepared. I had spent nine years in a den of iniquity feeling as if I had to do my best and ignore the status of the environment that surrounded me just to survive. This was a self-sabotaging mindset that kept me stuck in tormenting cycles which allowed people to take all the credit for my hard work and discredit me in the process. My faith was placed in the wrong place, and I learned my lessons as time progressed man proved to me how untrustworthy, manipulative, envious, cold, and damning their nature truly is. Going through the micromanagement, nepotism, nit picking, petty staged incidents, deceitful tattle tailing of certain co-workers to management behind my back in efforts to diminish my reputation for fear of my being promoted, and seeing certain management sit in secret meetings and speak falsely against me to also accomplish keeping me suppressed from promotion was all a graduation. This was the final piece of the puzzle and I worked toward finding a good balance for everything I was now focusing on for my life with divine knowledge and purpose at the forefront. In conversation with the Creator, I asked are you well pleased with me, and the answer given was *YES*. The key was searching and seeking the truth and giving my life in supplication as the *vessel* through which **good *works and miracles*** would come to pass. I had successfully transitioned from stagnancy to movement (which the transition forward is not easy, and the opposition will try to block you in every part of life to keep you stuck), did and was continuing the work on myself, and all while fulfilling the instructions sent by divine guidance. Most importantly I exercised **gratefulness and gratitude** **(The Spiritual Law of Gratitude)** with everything in my life and studied the **Universal Spiritual Laws**. I truly am grateful to know how much I am loved by my Creator and have the honor of seeing the **DIVINE VISION** bloom before me. There are no words that will ever be able to express how happy I am in my skin. Yes, the way to this happiness and peace can be paved with hardships, heartbreaks, setbacks, continuous self-work/discovery, healing, and finally deepening the connection with the Creator but it is all worth it! Do I still find myself being triggered every now and again, yes, but I remember to practice mindfulness and address the heart of the triggering by affirming and speaking life to myself! Now, I no longer feel the need to have to be with someone to be a success, or pressure from a ticking clock with every year that passes, or the need to be validated from anyone, or that I am not worthy. I received my Creators promises directly, have felt the joy and happiness to come, and I am secure in those promises as I continue to move in obedience. The most important lesson I have learned along my journey is that I am **ENOUGH** and **my belief** in this gives me the **confidence that I lacked** when I did not. I have received validation from the highest authority, my **CREATOR**. It all falls to **your free will, your choice, and your actions**.

In this period of **"planting good seeds"** and waiting I am assured that my Creator is well pleased with my progress. Being still in this knowledge gives me a peace that I cannot describe and, on those days, where it seems like the world is throwing all it possibly can to block me on my path I go to that peaceful place, remember who validates me, and the promises made for me. Finally, I am at a point in life that I can enjoy myself and be happy in the present before moving onto another adventure. This is where I choose to invest my time and energy, into maturing, and developing myself with divine grace and finally live. Once I made the decision to include the Creator and be used as the vessel for good works that is when I saw the most significant changes. Everyone's path is also not the same, what is the way of Yeshua for me may be the way of Buddha for someone else, and so on and so forth. The principal, however, is universal acknowledgement of the existence of a higher power, committing to seeking a deeper connection\what is true, walking the paths of the steps divinely ordered for you, and being grateful for all one has. This has brought me to the most peaceful and humbled place in life as I continue to grow and evolve according to *DIVINE WILL!*

This period of waiting has also presented its tests and trials. Disturbing family secrets which were thought to be dead and buried came to light. People from my past slowly started creeping up. I worked on my personal and business projects while dealing with the fall out of the layoff. However, I found a balance for my family, myself, and my deepened connection to the Creator. So many different things had risen now presenting their own challenges and distractions in place of my working for nine plus hours a day punching someone's clock. However, again because I am now choosing to learn from each situation that I may go through one thing sticks out to me now more than ever and that is one of the most important things I must remain focused on which is the *DIVINE PLAN* I have been armed with by now knowing. This knowledge keeps me grounded in moving forward through life dedicated to making strides and accomplishing what I was meant to. So, I am prepared to keep going and moving in my mission regardless of any distractions, obstacles, or deterrence's that may present themselves in the effort to take me off track.

I have accepted the fact that I am different. The reason I have felt that I do not fit in is because I do not. The layers that were placed on me for so long with the mindsets and false beliefs have been stripped allowing me to see who I truly am which has allowed me to change my mindsets and beliefs to honor myself & my Creator. This work will be constant throughout life, and I have chosen to dedicate myself to continue working on myself instead of putting my head down and allowing my decisions and plan for my life to be dictated by no one other than the Most High. This is also why the children being born now also have this attitude as they are prepared from before birth to come in honoring themselves. They are the rebuilders and the re-shapers of the world as we know it and as such will need an iron clad will to face the forces that are dead set against change in another direction. Children are coming with the knowledge of who they will be, and we can see it in child prodigies that are show cased in music, the sciences, the arts, business, and specifically technology. Coding is now a part of learning between the grades of five through twelve whereas back in my time of school we were only just learning about what computers were. This is just one of the paradigms that is currently shifting. Loads of information that was previously only available to select circles has now become known and available to us all for enlightenment and guidance on our individual paths of this grand design called life. My position prior to now was being torn and fighting against where I was being guided to go by staying in comfort zones like my work or toxic mindsets or being around certain people, which all contributed to holding me back. Essentially, I was fighting against myself, and it took the layers built over me being stripped for me to finally stop fighting, come into peace with myself through placing trust and faith in my Creator, allowing the Divine to validate me instead of seeking that from my environment, and believing in myself as my Creator believes in me to fulfill the will of my purpose. Therefore, I was called to write this book because the message is truly clear. We are being called back to the source of all creation which requires trust, obedience, belief, and choice. The choice to continue as we have lived which is based on a false imprisonment system or to free ourselves from those things that are ultimately taking precious time while pushing us further away from our one true love that provides purpose, enlightenment, and fulfillment. The choice to deny who we truly are inside putting on the masks society has trained us to or return to our truth and live authentically in our sovereignty as children of the Highest Authority. Feelings of being alone, not understood, cast aside, blamed, and not good enough are created when the choice is made to go against who we are and put-on false masks to play a part in the World Stage. For those who are experiencing whirlwind life changes of disappointment, setbacks, unjustified prejudice, depression, and traumatic pain from the past these are the symptoms of playing a role that is not the true plan for you. There is a reason we are all born with specific strengths, weaknesses, talents, gifts, and go through certain experiences but it takes facing ourselves in the good and bad, taking the journey of discovering who we are, making peace with that, and placing faith in the power that created us to put all the pieces of the puzzle together and successfully move forward while understanding you are connected to it all *(The Law of One)*. Your biggest asset is yourself and your connection to the Divine. We are all given a choice and mine was choosing to wake up from the illusion of life that I was submerged in. I chose to look inside myself *(Inner*

Knowing), see the false beliefs and mindsets, change them, acknowledge my truth, and stand in that. The moment this shift took place I was targeted more, placed through situations that would break anyone, and yet somehow, I am still here intact. When I became awake to the illusions of this life and started to make the changes to honor myself instead of sacrificing myself, I lost many so-called friends along the way, was able to forgive myself, able to love myself, and start living authentically as who I truly am not what one pretends to be. This is not the easiest decision or way of life because it requires cold hard truth and death of the *EGO (The I)*. Can I step outside the box that I have put myself in, can I face the unknown, and can I believe in myself? There are all new challenges to face on the way once you are awake but again the choice is in your hands to keep doing the work or fall back into allowing your life to be imprisoned, comfortable with the imposed conditioning of a false reality, and being at war with yourself.

Chapter 6 – Principals Used on My Journey for Self-Work & Development

(To be used with workbook)

There is no set blueprint for self-mastery, enlightenment, spiritual awakening, existential crisis, and or any other pivotal places in life. What I have found helpful on my Journey is first being aware of what is occurring in your life and taking accountability by doing the work necessary to elevate yourself to the next phase. Be creative and tailor your own healing and development process through your own process of seeking knowledge and self-discovery.

Here are some key methods I used practical application with on my journey to help:

A. *Recognizing that all is not well and the need to get to work!*

- Move away from any influences such as friends, co-workers, family members, and anything consuming time that is not in service to your highest good. (spend more time alone)
- Get plenty of rest.
- Make healthy diet changes incorporating more magnesium, water crest\rich greens, and get moving (exercise).
- Get into nature.
- Ask questions such as why I feel this way, why is my life this way, and what is my purpose. Also incorporating mindful quiet meditation!
- Create a sacred space or a place where you can be alone without distractions to pray, meditate, reflect,

research, organize, and be creative. *("Seek & You Shall Find")*

B. *Self-Reflection!*

- Review old Journals to look at your state during different stages of life, mindsets, and how have they helped or deteriorated progression. If you are a person who has not engaged in this practice start a journal to record your most inner thoughts as this is a way of connecting with yourself. Document anything of significance throughout your day such as something that triggers anger, annoyance, negative thinking, or even bad habits such as cursing. Then after a period of about one week review your findings, see if you can identify any self-sabotaging beliefs, chatter in your mind, or anything negative and look for the root of what may have caused them to be there.

- Things to look for when documenting are anything of significance such as things that draw your attention, for example a symbol that may have caught your eye while driving, or the color of an object on your desk, any triggered feelings, or mindsets that may cause certain thoughts in your mind.

- Document your strengths & weaknesses. Focus on how you can improve on your weaknesses!

- Identify what you want vs. what others may enforce or ask you to adhere to. Does the status quo in your life align with who you are, what you want, and your purpose or mission once identified!

- Identify repetitive toxic life cycles, learn your lessons, and move forward by breaking them with the wisdom you have acquired.

   > EG. For me this was seeing basically the same circumstances in most of my relationships from past to present that showed me I was over giving myself and engaging in unhealthy relationships vs. healthy relationship which is reciprocated with both parties and not just one person giving mostly everything or carrying the relationship. This was true in both acquaintances, friendships, and romantic relationships!

C. *Research*!

- Google, find studies, use library or university resources to explore different techniques to help you with getting in touch with yourself. Some examples include inner child therapy, types of abuse, different personality types or archetypes, Reiki, Yoga, different philosophy concepts, different Historical accounts such as the Egyptian, Roman/ English/ Russian Dynasties and or their equivalents in different cultures, the Bible/Torah/Koran/Pali Canon or equivalents in different religions, self-help literature such as "the 48 laws of power", phycology concepts, self- love literature, and any other topics that appeal to you. I got pulled down many rabbit holes with seeking information and your inner compass will do the same for you.

- Do an occasional reality check in by looking at the news only once a week to stay abreast of current events and reflect on it.

D. *Accepting the need for change and taking leaps of faith!*

- Identify that you may have to look at everything surrounding you & make changes:

Environments - Personal & Work

This involves you making serious assessments of every environment you place yourself in to include your home, career path, and social circles. Identify what and who is honoring to you and in service to your highest good while cutting away from your life any person, place, or thing that is not honoring to you or in service to your highest good. Decide if you may need to move locations where you live, change jobs or become your own boss, and remove people (friends & family) that are not reciprocators of your invested time and energy.

- Find your tribe:
  Identify persons & environments that are like minded, support you, your growth, and immerse yourself in that creating a new environment and fellowship circle that support you and your growth.

- Change **MINDSETS** or **BELIEFS** that are hindering to your soul growth & life progression:
  Look at your religious beliefs, raised or taught beliefs (generational), mindsets on making money, your outlook on love and relationship, and determine how they have impacted your decisions and outcomes in your life! Identify if it may be time to change some for ones that will serve the elevation your soul growth, and life progression.

  EG. One big change in mindset for me was going from feeling like I was a drop in the bucket to knowing I am a prize meaning I am enough despite anyone that may try to compete. I had to put myself in the frame of mind that there just is no completion regarding who I am, my worth, and what I have to offer.

- Self-Care & Love:
  Take your time & energy and invest it in yourself. This may mean putting yourself above engagements, people, and even your career path! Do things for yourself that you would expect from others. This may mean starting self-care regimens for your body, taking breaks for retreat time to disconnect from the

hustle\bustle of home and work life, spending time building that business idea you had for years, attending self-improvement seminars, and most importantly learning the art of ***LETTING GO***. Letting go can be anything you may be holding onto in your life that is tying or keeping you stuck on a life path such as a career, relationship, the past, fear, anxiety, or an organization that does not invest in you, your soul growth, or contribute to the fulfillment of your purpose or life mission. Make decisions that honor you, your purpose, and life mission. Engage in things that spark your creativity like hobbies, try new things, or engage in past times you stopped doing such as biking, gardening, music, or sports. When you incorporate a good amount of your time into yourself this is what helps bring you into alignment with your purpose or mission. Everything that is you reflects and tells you about who you are once you can connect the dots to include why you have certain talents, hobbies, past times, goals, and even spiritual gifts. Spend time getting in tune with yourself, sometimes that may mean revisiting yourself as a child, looking at the world through your childlike eyes, and comparing that to your adult eyes. You may even be able to identify if you should seek professional assistance or guidance from a licensed professional to address deep seeded trauma from your past to help you move on in your life. Purge yourself from negative practices, attachments to your energy, people, places, programming, and things that are not serving you. This can be accomplished in many ways on your own such as taking a spiritual bath, using salt or the ocean in declaration to remove all that does not serve your good from you and your life, use natural tools such as crystals & sage to cleanse yourself, home, and environments where you spend most of your time. If purging and cleansing is a concept that is a bit difficult to tackle on your own you can seek the assistance of a trustworthy professional spiritual leader, phycologist, or anyone in the professional position to assist.

- Mindfulness:
Be present in every moment, do not let your circumstances distract you to the point where you cannot even notice where you are, and the true nature of what is going on around you. Things are not always as they seem and because of a lack of awareness you may miss the little things that can either inspire great change or prevent catastrophic decisions. Practice being aware always! There are signs all around you that to the normal eye is missed. However, when your spiritual eye is open, and you are aware you will pay attention to the fish symbol on the car bumper in front of you in traffic or a number sequence will catch your attention in time or number sequences. The way things play out will have deeper meaning. You will understand why certain persons were sent into your life. You will start to learn from your past mistakes and use that knowledge in recognizing future issues. Your outlook

on the world will drastically change because you start to see the truth on many levels!

- Discernment:
  There is a great debate about this because some people may say that it makes you a judgmental person. However, when you have learned to listen to that still soft voice in you or pay attention to the urge in the pit of your stomach that makes you feel like something or someone is off, or trust what your spiritual senses have revealed a situation, person, place, or thing this is highly honoring to yourself and being obedient to higher guidance which serves your highest good! When you have mastered this, you will be able to see through any illusion that may be placed before you.

- Be Mysterious:
  Your journey is your own and you will have to develop the ability to keep what you are doing for yourself to yourself until the right time depending on what you are doing. I say this because you will find when applying some of these principles that not everyone in your circle or environment serves your highest good. The true nature of people, places, and things will be revealed to you and the art of mystery/being private is the best way to protect yourself and your growth.

- Believe in yourself:
  According to the bible man was made in the image of
  God! This means you are a masterpiece made in the
  image of what we know as the greatest power ever
  known and speaks volumes as to how powerful each
  one of us truly is. From a scientific point of view the
  mind of Man sets us apart from any animal species
  and makes us unique. The point is you are special,
  worthy, capable, and unlike any other. You are
  uniquely you. When you really acknowledge this
  truth and accept it in your heart this will build
  confidence in yourself. Belief is one of the key
  elements in every great person, place, or thing in
  creation! Affirm yourself, build your confidence,
  work on your weaknesses, be determined, make the
  necessary cuts for things not in service to you, learn
  your lessons, use the wisdom gained, and never give
  up. Stand for yourself in the full power of your
  authentic self and not what the world says you are.
  Self-mastery is the first step to unlocking the rest of
  your life!

- Be Still:
  Once you have come into the space where you
  believe in yourself, the talents given to you from the
  Creator, and have faith that the Creator has provided
  all that you need in you then everything else will fall
  into place in its right time. Being still occurs during
  the time you come into this awareness and the right
  time – *DIVINE TIME*. This time in between is where
  you can practice "Mindfulness" at its best, great

fullness or gratitude for everything you have received on your journey, and rest through knowing that all is working out for your highest good being at peace within who you are.

Acknowledgement of Influential Works \ Books of Interest:

- The Game of Life & How to Play It by Florence Scovel Shinn
- The Secret by Rhonda Byrne
- A Woman's Influence by Tony A & Sheri Gaskins
- Kingology by RC Blakes
- Queenology by RC Blakes
- The Art of Being Private Building in Silence by Daphne Madyara
- The Holy Bible
- The Laws of the Universe & The Bible: A Practical Guide to Abundant Living by Lori Kostenuk
- The 48 Laws of Power by Robert Greene
- Good Morning, I Love You: Mindfulness and Self-Compassion Practices to Rewire Your Brain for Calm, Clarity, and Joy by Shauna Shapiro PhD, Shauna Shapiro, et al.
- Healing Your Emotional Self: A Powerful Program to Help You Raise Your Self-Esteem, Quiet Your Inner Critic, and Overcome Your Shame by Beverly Engel
- The Discipline of Spiritual Discernment by Tim Challies
- Spiritual Discernment and the Mind of Christ by Francis Frangipane
- The Discerner: Hearing, Confirming, and Acting on Prophetic Revelation by James W. Goll
- Spiritual Warfare and The Discernment of Spirits by Dan Burke
- Empaths & Narcissists by Judy Dyer

- POWER: Surviving and Thriving After Narcissistic Abuse: A Collection of Essays on Malignant Narcissism and Recovery from Emotional Abuse by Shahida Arabi
- The Narcissist in Your Life: Recognizing the Patterns and Learning to Break Free by Julie L. Hall
- Angel Intuition: A Psychic's Guide to the Language of Angels by Tanya Carroll Richardson
- Are You an Earth Angel? Understand Your Sensitive & Empathic Nature & Live with Divine Purpose by Tanya Carroll Richardson
- Self-Care for Empaths: 100 Activities to Help You Relax, Recharge, and Rebalance Your Life by Tanya Carroll Richardson
- The Empath's Survival Guide: Life Strategies for Sensitive People By Judith Orloff MD
- The Book of Joy: Lasting Happiness in a Changing World by Dalai Lama & Desmond Tutu
- Mindfulness for Beginners: Reclaiming the Present Moment and Your Life (Book & CD)) by Jon Kabat-Zinn Ph.D.
- The Lineage of the Codes of Light by Jessie E. Ayani
- An Ascension Handbook by Tony Stubbs
- Mary Magdalene Revealed by Meggan Watterson
- The Red Lion by Maria Szepes
- Angel Prayers by Kyle Gray
- Spiritual Alchemy by Jenny Tyson

Youtubers of Interest:

- Breeny Lee -
  https://www.youtube.com/c/BreenyLee/featured
- Daphne Madyara -
  https://www.youtube.com/user/dephnedle
- Toney Gaskins -
  https://www.youtube.com/user/TonyGaskins
- Heather Lindsey -
  https://www.youtube.com/channel/UC3eXhhNTYTPv
  FsGE20gxk-w
- Grace for Purpose -
  https://www.youtube.com/channel/UCI8gcSTo1Fow
  sRJdilsjsZw
- Ralph Smart -
  https://www.youtube.com/user/Kemetprince1
- Aaron Doughty -
  https://www.youtube.com/channel/UC48MclMZIY_E
  aOQwatzCpvw
- Leeor Alexandra -
  https://www.youtube.com/c/LeeorAlexandra
- Justin Perry -
  https://www.youtube.com/c/YouAreCreators/featur
  ed
- Isabel Palacios -
  https://www.youtube.com/c/IsabelPalacios
- Erin on Demand -
  https://www.youtube.com/channel/UCN0UL-
  WYN5h8qKpywD1x5kg

- Dr. Romani - https://www.youtube.com/user/DoctorRamanDurvasula
- Stephanie Lyn - https://www.youtube.com/channel/UCAm2Q5XaKAkHSK-SZStujVg
- RC Blakes Jr. - https://www.youtube.com/channel/UCYaL9W8FyHSeiu9OuJ0lEvw

Websites of Interest:

- https://lonerwolf.com/
- https://www.psychologistworld.com/
- https://internationallightworkersassociation.com/
- https://www.americanempathassociation.com/
- https://www.edx.org/

CONTACT INFORMATION

Social Media:
Facebook – @TheJourney2Self or (12) Kristin Krigger | Facebook
Instagram – the.journey.toself or kristin.krigger
Twitter – @TheJtoSelf or @KristinK_Brand
Indeed – www.linkedin.com/in/kristin-k-81b1791bb

Mailing Address
Kristin M. Krigger
P.O. Box 502951
St. Thomas, US Virgin Islands 00805

Email Address
kristin.krigger@hotmail.com